Manifesto of New Realism

SUNY series in Contemporary Italian Philosophy
Silvia Benso and Brian Schroeder, editors

MANIFESTO OF NEW REALISM

Maurizio Ferraris

Translated by Sarah De Sanctis
Foreword by Graham Harman

Published by State University of New York Press, Albany

Printed in the United States of America

For information, contact State University of New York Press, Albany, NY
www.sunypress.edu

Production by Ryan Morris
Marketing by Anne M. Valentine

Library of Congress Cataloging-in-Publication Data

Ferraris, Maurizio, 1956-
[Manifesto del nuovo realismo. English]
Manifesto of new realism / Maurizio Ferraris ; translated by Sarah De Sanctis ; foreword by Graham Harman.
pages cm. — (SUNY series in contemporary Italian philosophy)
Includes bibliographical references and index.
ISBN 978-1-4384-5377-4 (hc : alk. paper) 978-1-4384-5378-1 (pb : alk. paper)
ISBN 978-1-4384-5379-8 (ebook) 1. Realism. 2. Philosophy, Modern—21st century. 3. Postmodernism. I. Title.
B835.F4713 2014
149'.2—dc23

2014002036

10 9 8 7 6 5 4 3 2 1

Suppose there is a black rock on an island, and that its inhabitants have come to believe—through elaborated experiences and an intensive use of persuasion—that the rock is white. Yet the rock would be black, and the inhabitants nothing but idiots.

—Paolo Bozzi (1930–2003)

CONTENTS

FOREWORD

GRAHAM HARMAN

In the book now before you, Maurizio Ferraris makes a lucid and sophisticated call for a realist turn in continental philosophy. Until lately, the word "realism" was almost never spoken aloud in the continental tradition. Or as Manuel DeLanda once put it, "for decades admitting that one was a realist was equivalent to admitting [that] one was a child molester."[1] Analytic philosophers have always had the option of bluntly defending the existence of a reality lying outside society, language, or the mind. But among continentals, to adopt an explicitly realist (or even *anti*realist) position was always to mark oneself as intellectually awkward. Beginning with phenomenology, and continuing in its ultra-hip French successors, the usual method was to treat the realism/antirealism problem as a "pseudo-problem." The mind was always already outside itself in intending objects, or Dasein was always already thrown into a world, even though this world and its objects were said to exist only as correlates of human beings.[2] Such maneuvers reputedly took us beyond realism and idealism alike, pointing to a new "third way," as in Merleau-Ponty's talk of an in-itself-*for-us*.[3] Only in 2007 did Lee Braver finally call a spade a spade with his blatantly *anti*realist account of the history of continental philosophy.[4] The fact that Braver's book has not prompted similar candor among his fellow antirealists suggests that continental philosophy is not yet willing to give up its traditional game of pretending to be neither realist nor antirealist. Even as formidable a thinker as Slavoj Žižek tells us with a straight face that materialism means the external world does not exist—*and* that he is not an idealist![5]

Until recently, it often seemed to me that the initial realist turn in continental philosophy came in 2002, with the publication of DeLanda's *Intensive Science and Virtual Philosophy* and my own debut book, *Tool-Being*.[6] But in saying so, I did inadvertent injustice to Maurizio Ferraris, whose works in Italian were unknown to me. Ferraris not only made the realist turn at an earlier and lonelier date than DeLanda and the speculative realists but took some personal risk in doing so. Born in Turin in 1956, Ferraris was a student of Gianni Vattimo and coauthor of Jacques Derrida,[7] two thinkers of a conspicuous antirealist stripe (despite various revisionist attempts to portray Derrida as a realist). In March 1992 Ferraris sat in Naples, listening to Hans-Georg Gadamer say that "being is language."[8] In a flash he realized that this was false, and the realist turn of Maurizio Ferraris commenced. Without success he urged Derrida to adopt a weaker textualist position, based on the principle that there is nothing *social* outside the text. In later years, as Italy sank into the mire of Silvio Berlusconi, it seemed to Ferraris that postmodern relativism had reached its logical outcome in right-wing populism, providing new *political* grounds for Ferraris to reject his former relativist position. Unsurprisingly, this led to dispute with his former teacher Vattimo, a vehement political opponent of Berlusconi but also one of the leading champions of postmodernist relativism.

In the new atmosphere of Anglophone continental thought, realism is not just a viable option but is arguably home to the most promising innovations of our time. Ferraris will serve as a welcome new influence. After years of being relatively unknown to the reader of English, he now has four books in our language: the present manifesto, the wonderful *Documentality*,[9] *Where Are You?*[10] and his bluntly titled *Goodbye, Kant!*[11] Ferraris once gave a brazen lecture under that title in Heidelberg, one of the citadels of classic German thought. While presumably he was most worried about how Gadamer might react, a more important listener for Ferraris that day was the young student Markus Gabriel, destined to be his future new realist colleague. Gabriel has described that Heidelberg lecture as having awakened him from something like an antirealist slumber.[12] Perhaps you, too, dear reader, will be awakened from slumber by the gentle harangues and urbane precision of Maurizio Ferraris.

NOTES

1. Manuel DeLanda, personal communication, January 30, 2007.
2. Thus, Quentin Meillassoux famously defines recent continental philosophy as "correlationism." See Meillassoux, *After Finitude*, trans. R. Brassier (London: Continuum, 2008).
3. See Maurice Merleau-Ponty, *Phenomenology of Perception*, trans. C. Smith (London: Routledge, 2002), 82–83.
4. Lee Braver, *A Thing of This World: A History of Continental Anti-Realism* (Evanston, IL: Northwestern University Press, 2007).
5. The first claim can be found on page 97 of Slavoj Žižek and Glyn Daly, *Conversations with Žižek* (Cambridge, UK: Polity Press, 2004). The second comes from page 36 of Slavoj Žižek, *The Ticklish Subject: The Absent Center of Political Ontology* (London: Verso, 1999).

6. Manuel DeLanda, *Intensive Science and Virtual Philosophy* (London: Continuum, 2002); Graham Harman, *Tool-Being: Heidegger and the Metaphysics of Objects* (Chicago: Open Court, 2002).
7. See Jacques Derrida and Maurizio Ferraris, *A Taste for the Secret* (Cambridge, UK: Polity Press, 2001).
8. Maurizio Ferraris, personal communication, August 5, 2013.
9. Maurizio Ferraris, *Documentality: Why It Is Necessary to Leave Traces*, trans. R. Davies (Bronx, NY: Fordham University Press, 2012).
10. Maurizio Ferraris, *Where Are You? An Ontology of the Cell Phone*, trans. S. De Sanctis (Bronx, NY: Fordham University Press, 2014).
10. Maurizio Ferraris, *Goodbye, Kant!* (Albany: State University of New York Press, 2013).
11. Markus Gabriel, personal communication, November 6, 2013.

PROLOGUE

In June 2012, at the Italian Institute for Philosophical Studies in Naples, I met a young German colleague, Markus Gabriel, who was planning an international conference on the fundamental character of contemporary philosophy. Markus asked what I thought could be the right title for such an event, and I replied to him, "New realism." It was a commonsensical consideration: the pendulum of thought that, in the twentieth century, oscillated toward antirealism in its various versions (hermeneutics, postmodernism, "linguistic turn," etc.) had moved, with the entry into the new century, toward realism (once again, in its many aspects: ontology, cognitive science, aesthetics as theory of perception, etc.).

To be precise, it was 1:30 p.m. on the 23rd of June when I coined the neologism. Yet it should not be taken as the inauguration of a new kind of theory: it was simply the title of a conference. "New realism," in fact, is not at all "my own theory," nor is it a specific philosophical current,[1] and it is not even a *koiné* of thought. It is simply a photograph (which I deem realistic indeed) of a state of affairs, as I believe was demonstrated several times by the vast debate that took place over the past few years.[2] With precisely the aim of underlining this circumstance, in the article in which I announced the conference on the matter,[3] I adopted the form of a manifesto or, rather, of *that* manifesto: "a spectre is haunting Europe." When Marx and Engels wrote this, it was not to announce *urbi et orbi* that they had discovered communism but rather to ascertain that communists were many. If, on the other hand, Kant had opened his *Critique of Pure Reason* stating "a spectre is haunting Europe: transcendental philosophy," they would have taken him for a madman, given that he was proposing a theory that, at that stage, only existed in his book.

The part of this work that does aspire to some kind of originality, or that at least I regard as a personal elaboration, is made up of the reflections I developed in the past twenty years and that I here summarize. The elaboration of realism, in fact, has been the main thread of my philosophical work ever since the turn that, at the beginning of the nineties, led me to abandon hermeneutics and to propose aesthetics as the theory of sensibility, a natural ontology as the theory of unamendability, and, finally, a social ontology as the theory of documentality.[4]

Therefore, to me the reference to realism has not been a means to boast of a laughable philosophical monopoly over the real, in a way that would not be too different from the claim of privatizing water. It has rather meant the affirmation that water is not socially constructed; that the sacrosanct deconstructive vocation lying at the core of any philosophy worthy of its name has to come to terms with reality, otherwise it will turn into a futile game; and that any deconstruction without reconstruction is irresponsibility.[5]

But, as I was saying, we must not forget the context in which I develop my considerations, which originate from a reflection upon the outcomes of postmodernism. What I call "new realism," in fact, is first of all the acknowledgment of a turn. The historical experience of media populisms, of post-9/11 wars, and of the recent credit crunch led to a severe denial of what I regard as the two dogmas of postmodernism: namely, that all reality is socially constructed and infinitely manipulable, and that truth is a useless notion because solidarity is more important than objectivity. Real needs, real lives and deaths, not bearing to be reduced to mere interpretations, have asserted their rights confirming the idea that realism (just like its opposite) not only has implications for knowledge but also for ethics and politics. Of course, this turn has not only a history but also—and first of all—a geography, circumscribed to what Husserl called "European spirit": that is, the West that Spengler prophesized the decline of ninety years ago. One can hardly imagine postmodernism in China or India. In any case, the part of the world I live in (which I believe I can claim to be a bit wider than the circle of my friends and acquaintances), namely, the West that experienced postmodernism, now seems to have abandoned it. How did this happen?

AUTHOR'S NOTE

In this short book, which was born out of the remains of many of my works taken up and elaborated here, I hope to have provided a clear—or at least concise—presentation of the reasons for my realism. I was able to test some of my arguments in two recent conferences: On the Ashes of Post-Modernism: A New Realism? (New York, Istituto Italiano di Cultura, November 7, 2011) and Nuovo realismo: una discussione aperta (Turin, Fondazione Rosselli, December 5, 2011). So I thank my colleagues who took part in them: Akeel Bilgrami, Ned Block, Paul Boghossian, Petar Bojanić, Mario De Caro, Roberta De Monticelli, Massimo Dell'Utri, Umberto Eco, Costantino Esposito, Paolo Flores d'Arcais, Markus Gabriel, Miguel Gotor, Andrea Lavazza, Diego Marconi, Armando Massarenti, Massimo Mori, Hilary Putnam, Stefano Rodotà, Riccardo Viale, Alberto Voltolini. I also thank my friends who read this text and helped me make it better: Tiziana Andina, Carola Barbero, Elena Casetta, Anna Donise, Daniela Padoan, Vincenzo Santarcangelo, Raffaella Scarpa, Enrico Terrone. Finally, a special thanks to Valentina Desalvo, to whom I owe the minting of a key term for my discourse: "realitism."

ONE

REALITISM

The Postmodern Attack on Reality

From Postmodernism to Populism

Postmodernism came into philosophy with a short book (109 pages) by the French philosopher Jean-François Lyotard, titled *The Postmodern Condition*, published in September 1979.[1] It was about the end of ideologies, that is, what Lyotard called "grand narratives": Enlightenment, Idealism, Marxism. These narratives were worn out; people no longer believed in them; they had ceased to move people's consciousness and justify knowledge and scientific research. It was a crisis, but (apparently) it was experienced with no tragedies, far from the dramas and guillotines of modernity, in an age that could not foresee what was soon going to happen from the Balkans to the Middle East, from Afghanistan to Manhattan. The ease with which the pandemic spread depended not only on what is so obscurely called "the spirit of the time" but precisely on the fact that postmodernism was carrying along a cosmopolitical crowd of forefathers:[2] the English historian Arnold Toynbee, who spoke about it in the forties; the German anthropologist Arnold Gehlen, who theorized "post-theory" in the fifties; the American novelist Kurt Vonnegut, who mixed black humor and science fiction in the sixties; the American architect Robert Venturi, who reinstated Las Vegas's Disney style at the beginning of the seventies. At the very beginning, in the thirties, there was even the Spanish literary critic Federico de Onís, who dubbed a poetic trend with that name.

The least common denominator of all these forerunners lies in the end of the idea of progress: the projection toward an infinite and undetermined future is followed by a retreat. Maybe the future is already here, and it is the sum of all pasts: we have a great future behind our backs. Yet, in the specific field of philosophy, we found a peculiar element, which we will tackle over and over in this book. Given that, in philosophy (and in knowledge in general), progress requires a trust in truth, the postmodern distrust in progress entailed the adoption of the idea—which finds its paradigmatic expression in Nietzsche—that truth can be evil and illusion good, and that this is the destiny of the modern world. The core of the matter is not to be found so much in the assertion "God is dead" (as Hegel claimed before Nietzsche) but rather in the sentence "there are no facts, only interpretations,"[3] because the real world ended up being a tale. A tale that reoccurs, according to the cyclic character of the eternal return instead of the linear becoming of universal history as the progress of civilization.

Thus far I have mentioned the strictly philosophical ideas. Nevertheless, unlike other trends and sects, and infinitely more than Plato's attempts in Syracuse—but also more than Marxism—postmodernism found a full political and social realization. The past few years, in fact, have taught us a bitter truth. That is, the primacy of interpretations over facts and the overcoming of the myth of objectivity took place, but they did not have the emancipative outcomes prophesized by professors. The "real world" never "became a tale"; there was no liberation from the constraints of reality—which is just too monolithic, compact, peremptory—nor was there a multiplication and a deconstruction of perspectives that seemed to reproduce, in the social world, the multiplication and radical liberalization of TV channels (as was believed in the seventies). The real world has certainly become a tale or, rather—as we shall see—it became a reality show; but the outcome was media populism, namely, a system in which (if one has such power) one can claim to make people believe anything. In news broadcasts and talk shows we did witness the realm of the "no facts, only interpretations" that—in what unfortunately is a fact and not an interpretation—then showed its true meaning: "the argument of the strongest is always the best."

Therefore, we now deal with a peculiar circumstance. Postmodernism is retreating, both philosophically and ideologically, not because it missed its goals but, on the contrary, precisely because it hit them all too well. The massive phenomenon—and, I would say, the main cause of the turn—was precisely this full and perverse realization that now seems close to implosion. The postmodernists' dreams were realized by populists, and in the passage from dream to reality, we truly realized what it was all about. So, the damage did not come straight from postmodernism—which was mostly animated by admirable emancipative aspirations—but by populism, which benefited from a powerful (although largely unaware) ideological support on the part of postmodernism. This had consequences that strongly affected not only the more or less vast elites that might be interested in philosophy but most of all a mass of people that never heard of postmodernism and that underwent the effects of media populism, including first and foremost the conviction that it is a system with no possible alternatives.

For this reason it is worth having a closer look at this realized and then overturned utopia by retracing the three crucial points in which I propose we summarize the postmodern *koiné*. First, *ironization*, according to which taking a theory seriously shows a form of dogmatism, and we should therefore maintain an ironical detachment toward our statements—expressed typographically by inverted commas[4] and even physically by flexing fingers to denote quotes in oral speech. Second, *desublimation*, namely, the idea that desire constitutes as such a form of emancipation, because reason and intellect are forms of dominion, and liberation must be looked for through feelings and the body, which are revolutionary *per se*.[5] And, most of all, *deobjectification*, that is, the assumption—whose catastrophic centrality will be shown throughout the book—that there are no facts but only interpretations, as well as its corollary for which friendly solidarity should prevail over an indifferent and violent objectivity.[6]

IRONIZATION

Postmodernism marks the entry of inverted commas in philosophy: reality becomes "reality," truth "truth," objectivity "objectivity," justice "justice," gender "gender," and so forth. At the base of this new quotation-marking of the world lay the thesis according to which the "grand narratives" (rigorously between quotation marks) of modernity or, even worse, ancient objectivism were the cause of the worst kind of dogmatism.[7] Rather than being fanatics, it is better to turn into "ironic theoreticians" who suspend the peremptoriness of any statement they make, seeing in facts, norms, and rules an evil *per se*. (Roland Barthes well represented the *Zeitgeist* when—only half-jokingly—he said that language is "quite simply fascist"[8] because it has semantics, syntax, and grammar.) The quotation mark, in its typographical variations, signifies a distancing that can also manifest lexical approximation, that is, inattentiveness, or an actual citation, that is, parasitism:[9] there is a reality built by others and we, as deconstructors, ironize on it, thinking we have thus done our job.

Quotation-marking is, in fact, a gesture similar to Husserl's *epoché*, to the suspension of judgment, to putting aside the existence of the objects under examination so as to grasp them in their phenomenic dimension. But compared to putting in brackets, putting between inverted commas is a very different strategy. Something that in Husserl was a philosophical exercise turns into a protocol of *political correctness* by which one proclaims that whoever dared remove the inverted commas would be performing an act of inacceptable violence or childish naïveté, claiming to be treating as real something that, in the best hypothesis, is only 'real' or "real."[10] This thesis, which implicitly turned into a fanatic whoever—although with full legitimacy—believed to possess some kind of truth, impeded (at least in the intentions) progress in philosophy, transforming it into a programmatically parasitic doctrine referring to science for any claim of truth and reality and limiting itself to quotation-marking. If then from the skies of theory we descend to the concrete realization of an "ironic theory" as the forever partial adhesion to our statements and beliefs, the consequences of ironization can be intuited by asking ourselves, for instance, what "an ironic postmodern witness" could be in a court where, instead of "equal justice under law," there was written "there are no facts, only interpretations." Leaving thought experiments aside and getting to real events, how little ironization entails emancipation is vastly demonstrated by the abuse of laughter, facetiousness, and farce in media populism, which instead provided a further confirmation of the ethological hypothesis that the facial expression of laughter is a legacy of the act of showing teeth—that, in animals, precedes aggression.

But what does the postmodern inclination for irony depend on? In a book that was very important to postmodernism, *Difference and Repetition*,[11] Gilles Deleuze claimed that one had to do for philosophy the same thing Duchamp did for art and propose a "philosophically bearded" Hegel just as Duchamp had drawn a moustache and a beard on the *Mona Lisa*. In his review of the book, Foucault went even further (he later took it back *in extremis*, as we shall see in chapter 4) affirming that thought had to become a masquerade.[12]

At a closer look, the ironic drive demonstrates that postmodernism has an ancient heart. Just as a star exploded long ago keeps irradiating its light, when postmodernism entered philosophy, at the end of the seventies, its cycle was coming to an end—a cycle that had its origin in Nietzsche's desperate radicalism, in the rebellion against systematic philosophy and in the various waves of philosophical avant-gardes that came one after the other in the twentieth century, and, even before that (as we shall see extensively in chapter 2), in Kant's Copernican revolution[13] (which truly was a Ptolemaic revolution, since it placed man at the center of the universe as a constructor of worlds through concepts). In this sense, postmodernism was not philosophical trash. It was the outcome of a cultural turn that largely coincided with modernity, namely, the prevalence of conceptual schemes over the external world. This explains the recourse to inverted commas as a means for distancing: we never deal with things in themselves but forever and only with mediated, distorted, improper phenomena that are therefore placeable between quotation marks. Nevertheless, what specifically characterizes postmodernism with respect to its predecessors and forefathers is that it is a programmatically parasitic movement. In art there is a venerable work of tradition and you draw moustaches on it, or you take a urinal or a soap pad box and declare it a work of art. In philosophy you take Plato and say he was antifeminist, or you take a TV series and say that it contains more philosophy than Schopenhauer's thought. More generally (thus completing a tendency that was already very well represented in much twentieth century philosophy), you proclaim that philosophy is dead, and that, at most, it consists of a kind of conversation or a writing genre that has nothing to do with truth or progress.

You might object that I am reducing postmodern theses, most especially its Ur-Thesis, "There are no facts, only interpretations," to a caricature. Yet, in the final analysis, this is the fundamental character of postmodernism, given that one is tempted to ask oneself: *what if the thesis consisted essentially of its own caricature?* If—in accordance with Duchamp's spirit—it consisted exclusively in emptying any argument out by turning thought into a masquerade? From this point of view, the genesis of weak thought (Pensiero debole)[14]—which I feel particularly entitled to talk about, as I have partly been involved in it and an eyewitness of it—seems paradigmatic. Scholars of different orientation and generations gather under a title of great evocative efficaciousness, but that is not truly constraining for anyone. What is being presented is not a theory but, indeed, an anthology with some valuable proposals that are nonetheless strongly dissonant. It manages to capture exactly the spirit of the time, which is that of impatience toward old academic stagnation and of the advance of media in public consideration. This perfect tuning is not limited to the national field, but it determines the international success of the homonymous book, so that little by little the very debate about *Weak Thought* leads to the persuasion that there is such a thing as "weak thought"—namely, a recognizable theoretical nucleus, or at least a "weak thought," a gust of the spirit of the time. The intimately ironic aspect of the proposal would have been even more evident had the volume carried a band saying "Ceci n'est pas une théorie." Yet, just like laughter, irony is not only detachment and nonviolence. In fact, the specific ironic theory of weak thought, as was precociously noted,[15] reproposed in more than one case the characteristics of a long period of Italian philosophy: suspicion toward science and technology, traditionalism, idealism. That is, suspicion toward realism (and the idea of progress in philosophy), always seen as a penalizing mistake with respect to the flights of thought. The ideal enemy of weak thought, then, was not the declared one (namely, dogmatism) but rather Enlightenment, that is, the claim of reasoning with one's own mind, as we shall better see in the last chapter of this book. De Maistre described the protestants' spirit as: "a spirit of cavil, envious to death of being in the right—quite natural, indeed, in every dissenter, but in Catholics wholly inexplicable."[16] In retrospect, weak thought shows the reappearance of the Catholic polemic against the *esprits forts*, against those who bring forward the absurd claim of being right. At the same time, there is deep skepticism and radical distrust toward mankind, which is seen as being in need of salvation and redemption, as well as incapable of following Rousseau's principle used by Kant as the epigraph of his work on Enlightenment:[17] "Wake up, my friend, and leave childish things behind!"

It is in this anti-Enlightenment climate that—with the complicity of irony and quotation marks—the misunderstanding takes place for which right-wing thinkers become left-wing ideologues, with a symmetric inverted phenomenon to the one for which rock music (initially perceived as left-wing) was easily adopted also by the far Right. The case of Heidegger as an antimetaphysical resistant, whose organic membership to Nazism is often forgotten or underestimated, is paradigmatic in this sense. Let me offer one example out of the many possible ones. Opening his contribution to the booklet *Ragione filosofica e fede religiosa nell'era postmoderna* [Philosophical reason and religious faith in the postmodern era],[18] Vattimo writes that Heidegger "also made a series of 'political mistakes,' such as his adhesion to Nazism." Now, one wonders why Heidegger's adhesion to Nazism is a political mistake between inverted commas, as if it were a weak mistake, perhaps not even a mistake and only a "stupidity"—*eine Dummheit*, as Heidegger described his adhesion to Nazism in his interview for the *Spiegel* in 1966.[19] The removal of his Nazism is due to many reasons, some of which are undoubtedly accidental or confused: for instance, the fact that Heidegger's philosophy was adopted, in France, also by thinkers very close to the left-wing, and that in general people were willing to trust the image of Heidegger's relation to Nazism that Heidegger himself had offered in his defense.

Among the numerous de-Nazification strategies,[20] in any case, none equals the plastic evidence of the *a priori* absolution (in which, once again, quotation marks play a central role) that can be found in the curator's note in the Italian edition of Heidegger's *Political Writings* that refers to the closing lines of the allocution dated May 17, 1933 where Heidegger wrote: "to our great Führer Adolf Hitler a German Sieg Heil." The curator's comment is: "Today the expression 'Ski Heil' is still used—with no political connotation whatsoever—by skiers to wish one another a good ski."[21] But, leaving the folklore aside, what was not seen (and provoked a semi-blindness about Heidegger's ideological tendencies) was that Heidegger's thought as a whole is hyper-hierarchic, and that the plea to nihilism and to the will to power, as well as the insistence on Decision and the abandonment of the traditional notion of "truth" constitute a deep and non-opportunistic adhesion to the *Führerprinzip*.

The condemnation of truth and objectivity as forms of violence and the consequent plea to an ironic pop theory thus elevate as their hero (with an undoubtedly objective irony) a philosopher that is certainly pop but utterly devoid of irony and very convinced of himself and his own "destinality."

DESUBLIMATION

The dialectics that manifests itself in ironization is also at work in the idea that desire can constitute an emancipative element *per se*. If Heideggerism is a right-wing movement that is adopted by the left-wing, with the desiring revolution we find a movement that—at least in the sixties and seventies—was primarily left-wing but that turned into an *instrumentum regni* for the Right. In fact, the history of populisms taught us how it is possible to develop a politics that is desiring and reactionary at the same time—after all, in line with significant precedents during the *Ancien Régime*, such as, for instance, the French aristocracy represented in Laclos's *Liaisons dangereuses* and censored by the Jacobins. There are therefore reasons to believe that, in its return to the Right, the desiring revolution rediscovered its genuine roots. Of course, the Nietzschean plea to the body and its "great reasons," or the critique of morals as a repressive and resentful structure, could be presented, for a while, as left-wing. Nonetheless, these elements were formed, in Nietzsche, within the frame of the theorization (that animates his entire thought) of a Dionysian revolution, where the "tragic man," antithetic to the rational man represented by Socrates, is first of all a desiring man.[22] The very recognition of the political role of the body, which is part of the theoretical horizon of the radical Left of the twentieth century, finds a full realization, but, again, in a reversed way: here it is the body of the leader that becomes an intensely political element.[23] Now, even without calling Nietzsche into question, it would have been enough to read Wagner's *Art and Revolution*[24]—written by a Wagner that seems to anticipate Marcuse—to understand that there may be a desiring revolution, but that it will still be a conservative revolution, given that desire, unlike reason, refers back to the archaic, to childhood, and to mothers.

In particular, in populism the conservative revolution manifests itself through the mechanism that was already extensively studied by Horkheimer and Adorno:[25] that of "repressive desublimation." The king concedes sexual freedom to the people and, in exchange, he keeps for himself not only the sexual freedom he gave to everyone else but also all the other kinds of freedom that he takes on as his exclusive privilege. The twist between body and desire is accompanied (in accordance with the anti-Socratism of the Dionysian revolution) by a diffused anti-intellectualism, which fosters the mirroring between the people and the king that constitutes the fundamental trait of populism. In other words, where at the dawn of postmodernism there was talk of the possibility of a desiring revolution, there takes place a desiring restoration, in the sense that desire is confirmed to be an element of social control. And it is not by chance that Foucault's change of mind that will lead him to take an antithetic position with regard to postmodernism started precisely from the issue of emancipative desire: four years after the *Anti-Oedipus*, with which in 1972 Deleuze and Guattari reaffirmed the link between desire and revolution, Foucault published *The Will to Knowledge*,[26] the first volume of the unfinished *History of Sexuality*, which substitutes the paradigm of emancipative desire for the thesis according to which sex is principally an instrument of control and exercise of authority, that is, the first and fundamental manifestation of "biopolitics"—which will be at the center of Foucault's reflections to follow.

Another aspect of the repressive desublimation is the authoritative use of the Nietzschean critique of morals. Under this profile, we discover that relativism, theorized by progressives and reproached by conservatives, was in fact much more practiced by the latter, in accordance with the paradoxes of the postmodernism-populism relation we are tackling. Consider, for instance, the apparently hyper-relativist argument of "what's wrong with it?"—which was often used as the standard answer to the criticisms toward the twists between sex and power. Now, in "what's wrong with it?" there intervenes a dispositive that hits the heart of a fundamental category of Enlightenment: that is, public opinion, which was born precisely as the place where the criticism of power would count as a means of control and guarantee of people's rights. Habermas[27] already described the transformation of public opinion, in the media world, from a place of debate to a place of manipulation of opinions on the part of mass media owners. But "what's wrong with it?" defines a third stage: namely, the fact that any surviving critical instance of public opinion is emptied *a priori* through the category of "moralism." Thus, "what's wrong with it?" presents itself as an incredibly efficacious instrument of repression of dissent and reaches its perfection when criticism is declassed to gossip. Here, too, there is an interesting mechanism. In fact, on the one hand, the charismatic personalization of power leads to the fact that all the attention is focused on the leader, his sphere and his behaviors—and this is so not due to a decision of public opinion but to a deliberate political choice typical of media populism. On the other hand, reciprocally, every criticism and dissent can now be reduced to gossip, and public opinion regresses to its pre-Enlightenment phase: that of resentful gossip on the bad costumes of the neighbors and the vices of the powerful.

DEOBJECTIFICATION

If, nevertheless, we look for the sufficient reason and the political engine of ironization and desublimation we find deobjectification: that is, the idea that objectivity, reality, and truth are a bad thing and even that ignorance is a good thing. Also in this case, postmodernism gathers at least three orientations of great cultural importance.

First of all, a Nietzschean tradition that offers multiple variations of the thesis according to which truth is nothing but an ancient metaphor, namely, a sort of myth or the manifestation of the will to power; that knowledge does not possess an autonomous emancipative value but rather constitutes an instrument of dominion or deceit, and, more radically, that there exists no such thing as "truth" but only a relationship of forces and struggles.[28] Then, the disappearance of the difference between myth and *logos*, or between real world and apparent world, produces a second effect: the recourse to myth, which traditionally was a right-wing patrimony, is recovered by the Nietzschean-Heideggerian Left, through the project of a "new mythology."[29] But the element that was by far the most ubiquitous (as it also involves a great part of twentieth-century analytic philosophy) was the one that proclaimed, with a radicalization of Kantism, that there is no access to the world if not through the mediation (which, in postmodernism, is radicalized and becomes construction) of conceptual schemes and representation.

We have a real case study on the perverse effects of deobjectification. In the mid-seventies, the epistemologist Paul K. Feyerabend affirmed that there is no privileged method for science, because in the confrontation between different scientific theories there are largely incommensurable worldviews set one against the other. In this frame, it is far from obvious that Galileo was right; rather, Bellarmine had all the rights to condemn Galileo's doctrine, which would have had negative repercussions on the asset of a society that found its ordering principle in the Church.[30] It is evident that, with such a statement, Feyerabend wanted to reject a strictly positivistic conception of physics, namely, the idea that knowledge consists of a mere collection of data needless of interpretations or conceptual schemes—and let us not forget that the context in which he expressed his position was intentionally provocative, since it was the *pars destruens* of *For and Against Method*, a book planned with Imre Lakatos and published posthumously in 1999. The outcome was that, twenty years later, Feyerabend's argument was used, in all seriousness, by Benedict XVI in order to affirm that epistemologists themselves claim that Galileo was not ultimately right, and most of all in order to articulate a discourse on the bases of which human knowledge leads to antinomies (like the one setting Galileo against Bellarmine), which can only find a solution in a superior form of rationality.[31]

This is postmodern dialectics at work. Deobjectification, while formulated with emancipative intentions, turns into the delegitimation of human knowledge and into the reference to a transcendent foundation. So, on the one hand, postmodern philosophers adhere to skepticism and have no ultimate reasons to justify Copernicus's superiority with respect to Ptolemy or Pasteur's with respect to Asclepius, because these are, anyhow, confrontations between conceptual schemes, as there is no "outside" reality. On the other hand—beyond the equivalence of things in the world and overcoming the inanity of learned quarrels—there opens up space for transcendence. Underlining "how deep the self-doubt of the modern age, of science and of technology goes today," the former pope easily recovers the prestige that the Church had lost when its worldview was contested by science. Once he is done with the defense, he can go on the attack by reproposing a *Weltanschauung* that is now doubly justified, both as a *legitimate* worldview like any other and therefore nonrejectable, and as a *more true* worldview, because it is founded "by its inscription into a greater reasonableness" and is therefore better compared to relativistic worldviews.

But the area where skepticism and the farewell to truth have shown their most aggressive side is politics.[32] Here, postmodern deobjectification was, exemplarily, the underlying philosophy of the Bush government, which theorized that reality was simply the belief of "reality-based communities"—that is, unwary people who do not know how things go. This praxis found its most concise expression in the response by one of Bush's consultants to the journalist Ron Suskind: "We're an empire now, and when we act, we create our own reality. And while you're studying that reality—judiciously, as you will—we'll act again, creating other new realities, which you can study too."[33] An arrogant absurdity, of course. Yet, eight years before that the philosopher and sociologist Jean Baudrillard had claimed that the Gulf War was nothing but a TV fiction,[34] playing (like Feyerabend) the role of the useful skeptic in favor of a cause that was certainly not his own.

From Realitism to Realism

The final outcome of the joint action of ironization, desublimation, and deobjectification can be called "realitism":[35] an entirely contingent name (as it refers to TV reality shows) that, nonetheless, captures the substance of that "world well lost"[36] in which postmodern thinkers saw the bright side of the age. Any authoritativeness of the real is cancelled, and, in its place, a quasi-reality is arranged with strong fictional elements, resting on three fundamental mechanisms. The first one is *juxtaposition*, for instance, in TV programs in which a report on atomic fission can be followed or preceded by one on reincarnation. The second is *dramatization*: you take something real and dramatize it with actors, turning it into a piece of semi-fiction. The third could be called *dreamization*: what is life in a reality show? Dream or reality? With this strategy, a fully realized postmodernism manifests itself as a violent and inverted utopianism. Instead of recognizing the real and imagining another world to realize instead of it, postmodernism regards the real as a tale and assumes that this is the only possible liberation: since there is nothing to realize and, after all, there is nothing to imagine, it is a matter of believing that reality is like a dream—harmless and fulfilling. Obviously, these three procedures can be combined with huge outcomes, exploiting the reality effect deriving from the use of the television medium and especially of news and reportages ("it must be true, TV said so"). Thucydides already put in historical characters' mouths discourses largely made up by him, but in the society of communication and recording there seems to be a change in status, due to the quantity of material online. The overall effect is to blur the dividing lines not only between reality and fiction but also between science, religion, and superstition.

As such, realitism is therefore not a simple postmodern product. It has an ancient heart, as old as mankind's desire for illusion, as well as the taste for mystification and its convenience. Thus, realitism appears in our mind in childhood, when we wonder whether things around us are real or whether we are dreaming, and it is developed in the tales through which we hope to change the world. *Per se*, realitism is merely a variant of solipsism: that is, of the idea that the external world does not exist, that it is a mere representation, perhaps even at our disposal. At first it seems like a moment of great liberation: the weight of the real is lifted and we can be the makers of our own world. Nietzsche saw in it the most beautiful liberation, the "bacchanal of free spirits," but it is hard to agree. If there is no external world, if there is no difference between reality and representation, then the prevailing mood will be melancholy or rather what we could define as a bipolar syndrome oscillating between a sense of omnipotence and the feeling of the pointlessness of everything. In the end, one feels lonely. The outside world does not exist; we are simply dreaming our dream or even someone else's dream: a programmed and almost expired one. In the eighteenth century, the Scottish philosopher Thomas Reid explained this with calm irony. If everything is a representation, then "the whole universe about me, bodies and spirits, sun, moon, stars, and earth, friends and relations, all things without exception, which I imagined to have a permanent existence, whether I thought of them or not, vanish at once."[37] And then the dream turns into a nightmare, like in *The Truman Show*.

What to do? Postmodernists have not been blind to the Golem they created—or at least philosophically sanctioned—precisely because, at the origin of their stance, there was a sincere emancipative desire and not a project of domination and mystification. But most of the time they adopted Wagner's strategy that "only the weapon that cast the wound can heal the wound"[38]—a sentence that is almost as risky as Hölderlin's "where danger grows, so does that which saves." Which is after all (let us note this) the fundamental principle of magical thought, according to which like cures like. Upon closer examination, and notwithstanding its insistence on irony and disillusion, postmodernism turns out to be a magical antirealism: a doctrine attributing to the spirit an uncontested dominion over the world. It is against this spirit that, with the turn of the century, realism came to the fore. It was a matter of relegitimizing—in philosophy, politics, and everyday life—a notion that, at the peak of postmodernism, was considered a philosophical naïveté as well as the manifestation of political conservatism, given that the appeal to reality, in ages still tied to the fatal slogan "all power to the imagination," seemed like the wish for nothing to change and the acceptation of the world for what it is. Thirty years of history taught us the opposite.

As I mentioned in the prologue, what I call "new realism" is therefore the common name of a transformation that hit contemporary philosophical culture and that was developed in many directions. First of all, the end of the linguistic turn and the stronger realist inclination of philosophers that, while not adhering to postmodernist positions, had previously been more sensitive to the reasons of constructivism and the modeling role of conceptual schemes upon experience. Think of Hilary Putnam's passage from "internal realism" to "commonsense realism,"[39] or of the claim of the importance of experience with respect to conceptual schemes in Umberto Eco,[40] or again of the development of a "speculative realism" by the younger generations of philosophers.[41] Another way in which the turn took place is the return to perception, which was traditionally neglected by philosophical transcendentalism culminating in postmodernism. Typically, the fact that aesthetics returned to be considered not as a philosophy of illusion but as a philosophy of perception[42] revealed a new openness toward the external world, namely, a real that lies beyond conceptual schemes and that is independent from them—just as it is impossible for us to correct optical illusions or change the color of the objects surrounding us by mere reflection. A third significant element of the realistic transformation is what I would call the ontological turn, namely, the fact that both in analytic and in continental philosophy there has been an increasing recovery of ontology as the science of being[43] and of the multiplicity of objects, which—from perception to society—constitute a research area that is not necessarily subordinated to natural science. With the return of ontology, therefore, there is the overcoming of the prevailing philosophical attitude ever since Kant, who had bid ontology farewell by claiming that philosophy had to cease dealing with objects (now pertinent to science) and give up the "proud name of an ontology" so as to merely investigate—under "the modest title of analytic of the pure understanding"[44]—the conditions of possibility of knowing these objects (namely, it had to set itself in favor of or against science).

Thus, this is the roughly sketched portrait of contemporary philosophy, which seems profoundly changed with respect to the situation we still found at the end of the last century. Nevertheless, as I anticipated in the prologue, what I will propose in the next three chapters is my personal conception of realism as I developed it in the past twenty years. I sum it up in three key words—Ontology, Criticism, Enlightenment—which react to the respective fallacies of postmodernism: the fallacy of being-knowledge, the fallacy of ascertainment-acceptance, and the fallacy of knowledge-power.

Ontology simply means: the world has its laws and imposes them, namely, it is not the docile colony on which to exercise the constructive action of conceptual schemes. The mistake made here by postmodern thinkers was due to the fallacy of being-knowledge, that is, the confusion between ontology and epistemology: between what there is and what we know about what there is. It is clear that in order to *know* that water is H_2O I need language, schemes, and categories. But that water *is* H_2O is utterly independent from any knowledge of mine—so much so that water was H_2O even before the birth of chemistry, and it would still be if we all disappeared from the earth. Mostly, as regards nonscientific experience, water wets and fire burns whether I know it or not, independently from languages, schemes, and categories. At a certain point, something resists us. It is what I call "unamendability": the salient character of the real. This can certainly be a limitation but, at the same time, provides us with the support that allows us to distinguish dreams from reality and science from magic. This is why I entitled the chapter dedicated to ontology "Realism."

Criticism, then, means this. With what I define as the "fallacy of ascertainment-acceptance," postmodernists assumed that ascertaining reality consists in accepting the existing state of affairs and that, inversely (although with a logical gap), irrealism is emancipative *per se*. Yet, it is clearly not so. Realism is the premise of criticism, while irrealism is at one with acquiescence, the tale we tell children so they fall asleep. Baudelaire noted that a dandy could have only spoken to the crowd in order to mock it.[45] Let alone an irrealist, incapable, for his own theories, of establishing whether he is *really* transforming himself and the world or whether, vice versa, he is simply imagining or dreaming about doing something of that kind. The realist, instead, has the possibility to criticize (if she wants to) and transform (if she can) by the virtue of the same banal reason why the diagnosis is the premise of therapy. And given that any deconstruction that is an end to itself is irresponsibility, I decided to entitle the third chapter "Reconstruction."

Finally, let us come to *Enlightenment*. Recent history confirmed Habermas's diagnosis that, thirty years ago, saw postmodernism as an anti-Enlightenment groundswell,[46] which finds its legitimacy in what I define "fallacy of knowledge-power," according to which behind any form of knowledge there hides a power experienced as negative. As a consequence, instead of mainly linking itself to emancipation, knowledge becomes an instrument of enslavement. This anti-Enlightenment is the heart of darkness of modernity: namely, the rejection of the idea of progress and of the trust in the link between knowledge and emancipation in great thinkers such as de Maistre, Donoso Cortés, Nietzsche, which is summarized in Baudelaire's idea that "Throne and altar" is a revolutionary maxim.[47] It is they that the postmodernism-populism time lapse seems to have proven right. Now, in order to exit this deep obscurity and to obtain the "Emancipation" that lends its name to the last chapter, it will thus be necessary to resort to Enlightenment, which, as Kant put it, is "sapere aude!" and marks "man's emergence from his self-incurred immaturity."[48] Enlightenment, today, still requires a stand and faith in mankind, which is not a fallen race in need of redemption but an animal species that evolves and that, in its progress, was endowed with reason.

TWO

REALISM

Things That Have Existed Since the Beginning of the World

The Fallacy of Being-Knowledge

Let us start with ontology and with the criticism of the fallacy of being-knowledge, because here lies the core of the whole debate on realism. Diego Marconi has characterized the opposition between realists and antirealists as an antithesis between two intuitions.[1] The first, the realist one, posits that there are things (for instance, the fact that there are mountains over four thousand meters tall on the moon) that do not depend on our conceptual schemes. The second (that Marconi calls "hermeneutical" or "Kantian") believes instead that the fact that there are over four thousand meter tall mountains on the moon is also dependent on our conceptual schemes or even simply on the words we use ("Could we truly say that there are mountains on the moon if we did not have the concept or word for 'mountain,' 'moon,' etc.?") I propose we call this intuition "constructionist" or "constructivist," as it assumes that relatively large parts of reality are constructed by our conceptual schemes and perceptual apparatuses.* In the next two chapters, which constitute the theoretical core of the book, I intend to discuss the genesis and the limits of the constructivist intuition, to compare it with the realist intuition, to determine the areas in which the constructivist intuition can be lawfully applied, and finally to propose a "treaty of perpetual peace" between constructivism and realism.

The fundamental argument of the constructivist intuition—namely, the fact that "somehow" (an expression that, not by chance, is very dear to constructivists) the existence of over four thousand meter tall mountains on the moon also depends on our conceptual schemes (or our language)—is clearly Kantian, constituting an application of the principle that "intuitions without concepts are blind."[2] Kant's statement has nothing inherently problematic *per se*, since there are many circumstances in which it can be easily applied, appearing fully justified: it is difficult to act meaningfully in scientific research or in political or social interaction if you are not equipped with concepts. The problem, though, is that Kant meant that concepts are necessary in order to have *any experience*, so that we need a concept even to slip on a patch of ice.[3] Which is not only false in itself, but also starts a process that leads to an absolute constructivism. Because if we assume that conceptual schemes have a constitutive value for any kind of experience, then, going one step further, we will be able to claim that they have a constitutive value for reality (at least if, following Kant, we assume there is a phenomenic reality in the world that coincides with the experience we have of it). At this point, with a full realization of the fallacy of being-knowledge, what there is seems to be determined by what we know of it.

---

*TN: These terms are used interchangeably throughout the chapter.

First of all, it is worth asking what has led philosophers to take such a risky and laborious path. The explanation can easily be found in one of the turns of modern philosophy, between Descartes and Kant, and this is why, elsewhere,[4] I have proposed we call the confusion between being and knowledge "transcendental fallacy." It is therefore reasonable to trace the fallacy back to the transcendental turn that has its remote origin in Descartes: "it is prudent never to rely entirely on things which have once deceived us."[5] Thus indeed spoke Descartes, in order to teach us to distrust the senses, those unreliable servants that have occasionally deceived us and of which then we shall systematically be wary. In line with this assumption, Descartes argues that certainty is not to be sought outside, in a world that is a forest of sense deceits, but inside, in the *cogito*: the home of clear and distinct ideas. In this choice there is something that—it is really appropriate to say this—hits the eye, namely, the abandonment of the natural attitude. We normally trust the senses, and if we happen to doubt them it is in special circumstances, for example, when we demand a 100 percent certainty. That is, when we submit nature to an *experimentum crucis*, and we invite it to say yes or no unequivocally, since according to Descartes we (as scholars, of course) must only deal with the objects we have a certain and indubitable knowledge of.

This hyperbolic request of knowledge, if transferred to experience, nevertheless turns into its opposite. We lose natural certainty and cannot replace it with a reliable scientific certainty, precisely because, by its own nature, science is progressive (and therefore never definitive). Being equally demanding in ordinary experience is thus not necessarily the right move, because instead of certainty we get irremediable doubts: if we ask of experience the same standard of certainty we require of science, we will end up being certain of nothing. The counterproof of this is provided by Hume, who became a skeptic precisely considering, just like Descartes, that inductive reasoning based on experience can never be 100 percent certain. And given that, for Hume, all knowledge comes from experience, and the real abyss is not between a 100 percent and 1 percent likelihood but between a 100 percent and 99 percent probability, then all the knowledge we have lies on a friable ground that offers no guarantee.

It is at this point that the Kantian moment takes place, with a move destined to mark all philosophy to follow: if every knowledge starts with experience, but if the latter is structurally uncertain, then it will be necessary to found experience upon science, finding *a priori* structures that can stabilize its uncertainty. To achieve this, we need a change of perspective: we have to start from the subjects rather than the objects and ask ourselves—in accordance with the matrix of all subsequent constructionism—not how things are in themselves but how they should be made in order to be known by us, following the model of physicists who question nature not as scholars but as judges: that is, using schemes and theorems. Kant then adopts an *a priori* epistemology, that is, mathematics, to found ontology: the possibility of synthetic *a priori* judgments allows us to fixate an otherwise fluid reality through certain knowledge. In this way, transcendental philosophy moved constructionism from the sphere of mathematics to that of ontology.[6] The laws of physics are mathematics applied to reality, and, in Kant's hypothesis, they are not the contrivance of a group of scientists, but they are the way in which our minds and senses work. Our knowledge, at this point, will no longer be threatened by the unreliability of the senses and the uncertainty of induction, but the price we have to pay is that there is no longer any difference between the fact that *there is* an object X and the fact that we *know* the object X. And since knowledge is inherently construction, there is no difference in principle between the fact that we know the object X and the fact that we *construct* it—just as in mathematics, where knowing 7 + 5 = 12 is equivalent to constructing the addition 7 + 5 = 12. Of course, Kant invites us to think that behind the phenomenal object X there is a noumenal object Y, a thing in itself inaccessible to us; but the fact remains that the sphere of being coincides to a very large extent with that of the knowable, and that the knowable is essentially equivalent to the constructible.

At the origin of the fallacy of being-knowledge there is therefore an interweaving of topics: 1) the senses deceive (they are not 100 percent certain); 2) induction is uncertain (it is not 100 percent certain); 3) science is safer than experience, because it has mathematical principles independent from the deceptions of the senses and the uncertainties of induction; 4) experience must then be resolved in science (it must be founded by science, or at worst, it must be unmasked by it as a misleading "manifest image"); 5) since science is the construction of paradigms, at this point experience will be construction too, namely, it will shape the world starting from conceptual schemes.

Here is the origin of postmodernism. Following and radicalizing Kant, constructionists will confuse, without residues (i.e., also abolishing the noumenon), ontology with epistemology: what there is (and is not dependent on conceptual schemes) and what we know (and depends on conceptual schemes). The two things, of course, are not the same, because the fact of knowing that this key lets me open the front door (epistemology) does not allow me to open the door if I have lost the key in question (ontology). Yet, as Alessandro Manzoni put it, these are "metaphysical subtleties, which never enter the mind of the multitude," or at least circumstances we do not mind if we take it as an undisputed dogma that the world "out there" (because of what we said in chapter 1, quotation marks are *de rigueur*) is a chimera and that the relationship with the world passes necessarily through conceptual schemes. *De facto*, with the combined action of this and the other two fallacies of postmodernism, the one of ascertainment-acceptance (for which knowledge is resignation) and that of knowledge-power (whereby knowledge is instead manipulation), we come to a complete discrediting of knowledge—a discrediting that has the ironical peculiarity of being caused and nurtured by professors who have made of it the subject of courses, books, and seminars.

The Slipper Experiment

But is this hyperbole really so inevitable? Of course not; and it is not hard to shout "the real is naked," that is, the real is not at all dressed with the dense network of conceptual schemes that constructionists wrap it up with. I can illustrate this through what I called "the slipper experiment," which I shall now report in the terms in which I presented it ten years ago as an anticonstructivist argument.

1. *People.* Take a man looking at a carpet with a slipper on it; he asks another to pass him the slipper, and the other, usually, does so without significant difficulty. It is a trivial phenomenon of interaction, but it shows very well how, if indeed the outside world depended even slightly not so much on interpretations and conceptual schemes but on neurons, then the fact that the two do not possess the *same* neurons should make the sharing of the slipper impossible. It might be objected that neurons do not have to be exactly identical in number, position, or connections; this, however, not only weakens the argument, but it contradicts evidence that is difficult to refute: the fact that differences in past experiences, culture, conformations, and brain equipment may lead to significant divergences at a certain level (does the Spirit proceed from the Father and the Son, or only from the Father? What do we mean by "freedom"?) is common knowledge, and it is the reason why there are disputes between different opinions. But the slipper on the carpet is another thing: it is external and separate from us and

our opinions, and it is therefore provided with an existence that is qualitatively different from the kind that we tackle, say, in discussing the status of issues such as euthanasia or preventive war. In other words, the sphere of facts is not so inextricably interwoven with that of interpretations. Dialogue can be important when there is a normative element at stake: in order to determine whether something is legitimate or not, it is better to have a look at what people think and debate the issue. But to determine whether the slipper is on the carpet, I merely have to look at it or touch it. In any case, discussing it would be of little help.

2. *Dogs*. Now let's take a dog that has been trained. He is told, "Bring me the slipper." And, again, he does so without encountering any difficulties, just like the man above, even though the differences between his brain and the man's are enormous and his understanding of "Bring me the slipper" may not seem comparable to that of a human. In fact, the dog does not ask himself whether the man is really asking him to bring the slipper or if he is quoting the sentence or using it in an ironic sense—while it is likely that at least some people would.

3. *Worms*. Now let's take a worm. It has no brain, nor ears; it has no eyes, it is far smaller than the slipper and only has the sense of touch, whatever such an obscure sense may mean. So we cannot say to it, "Bring me the slipper." However, crawling on the carpet, if it meets the slipper, it can choose between two strategies: either to turn around it or to climb over it. In both cases, it encounters[7] the slipper, although not quite like I encounter it.

4. *Ivy*. Then let's take ivy. It has no eyes, it has nothing whatsoever, but it climbs (or at least thus we express ourselves, treating it as an animal and attributing a deliberate strategy to it) up the walls as if it were seeing them or moves slowly away if it finds sources of heat that annoy it. The ivy will either bypass the slipper, or it will climb over it, not too unlike the

way a man would do in front of an obstacle of larger size, but with neither eyes nor conceptual schemes.

5. *Slipper*. Finally, take a slipper. It is even more insensitive than the ivy. But if we throw the slipper onto the other, it encounters it, much like it happens to the ivy, the worm, the dog, and the man. So it is really hard to understand in what sense even the most reasonable and minimalist thesis about the intervention of the perceiver upon the perceived can make some kind of ontological claim, let alone the strong ones. Also because one could very well not take another slipper but simply imagine that the first one is there, in the absence of any animal observer or without a vegetable or another slipper interacting with it. Would there be no slipper on the carpet, then? If the slipper is really there, then it must be there even if no one sees it, as is logically implied by the sentence "There is a slipper"—otherwise one could say, "It seems to me that there is a slipper" or, even more correctly, "I have in me the representation of a slipper," if not even, "I have the impression that I have in me the representation of a slipper." Consider that making the existence of things depend on the resources of my sense organs is *per se* not at all different from having them depend on my imagination, and when I argue that there is a slipper *only* because I see it I am actually confessing to having a hallucination.

These are the obvious circumstances hidden behind the fallacy of being-knowledge, for which we are all little physicists and chemists intent on constructing our own experiences just as we construct experiments in the laboratory. This fallacy opens a path taken by the vast majority of philosophers of the nineteenth and twentieth centuries. Calling one's revolution by the name of Copernicus, that is the scholar who—at least for modern consciousness—has taught us that the sun never really sets, is certainly misleading (since, indeed, Kant's revolution is rather Ptolemaic), but it means electing as a point of observation not what we see but what we know, and it especially means concluding that encountering a thing is basically the same as knowing it. The consequences are manifold and define the scene in which the modern and postmodern constructionist operates: what we see is made to depend on what we know; it is postulated that the mediation of conceptual schemes operates everywhere; and, finally, it is asserted that we never enter a relationship with things in themselves but always and only with phenomena.

Ontology and Epistemology

Unlike ancient skeptics, postmodern constructionists do not doubt the existence of the world; they claim it is constructed by conceptual schemes and that it is therefore amorphous and indeterminate in itself. This move seems much less binding, but since the constructionist (unlike the skeptic) identifies being and knowledge, then the outcome is just as powerful, although with sociologically different outcomes. The purpose of the skeptic, in fact, is to expose the vanity of human knowledge: his seminal text is the *Adversus mathematicos* by Sextus Empiricus, which could be translated as "against professors," given that it targets not only mathematicians but also grammarians, rhetoricians, surveyors, astrologers, and musicians—in short, all the arts of the *trivium* and the *quadrivium*. The constructivist opts for a diametrically opposite strategy, instead, exalting the function of the professor in the construction of reality: his seminal text is *The Order of Things* by Foucault, in which you can read that man is constructed by human sciences and might disappear with them.[8] If the skeptic aims at not being surprised by anything, the constructionist's end is wonder, and his crucial move is the removal of the obvious, that is, the formulation of *fashionable nonsense*,[9] of surprising claims that demonstrate the role played in the construction of experience by conceptual schemes and culture—that is, in the final analysis, precisely by professors.[10] Hence the claims that, following the fallacy of being-knowledge, give an exorbitant power to science, as has happened with the sociologist of knowledge Bruno Latour when he stated that Ramses II could not have died of tuberculosis because the bacilli responsible for the disease were only discovered in 1882.[11] This bizarre claim does not take into account that if the birth of a disease truly coincided with its discovery, we should immediately suspend all medical research, as we already have more than enough diseases: the true cause of the world's evils would turn out to be no longer Pandora (as we thought) but Asclepius. Then, the fact that professors do not love one another, and that—after attributing the construction of reality to knowledge—they claim (according to the fallacy of being-knowledge) that knowledge is an instrument of the will to power, is, after all, part of the way human things go. The ultimate outcome of constructivism is that of skepticism: the discrediting of knowledge.

It is not surprising, at this point, that the constructionist might also argue, both polemically and in partial good faith, that the only content of realism is the thesis: "reality exists." It is a bit exuberant as an argumentative move, not unlike that of someone who claimed that the only content of idealism is "there are ideas," the only content of nihilism "there is nothing," and perhaps the only content of communism "there are commons." In any case, however, *the realist does not merely say that reality exists. She supports a thesis that constructionists deny, namely, that it is not true that being and knowing are the same*, and that indeed between ontology and epistemology there exist several essential differences to which the constructionist does not pay attention. The constructionist claims that if fire burns, water is wet, and the slipper is on the carpet, it all depends on conceptual schemes.[12] It is clearly not so. It depends on the fact that fire burns, water is wet, and the slipper is on the carpet: these characters are ontological, not epistemological. In fact (think of the slipper experiment), there is no doubt that we relate to the world through conceptual schemes (whoever reads these lines must have learned the alphabet and must speak English), but this does not mean that the world is determined by our conceptual schemes. I can know (or ignore) all I want; the world is what it is.

It is extremely important not to confuse ontology and epistemology. Otherwise there will be the realm of "there are no facts, only interpretations," a principle according to which—as we have seen talking about "deobjectification" in chapter 1—it can be argued that Bellarmine and Galileo were both right, or even that Bellarmine was more right than Galileo, who therefore got what he deserved. This is clear proof of the fact that if we abandon the reference to an external world that is stable and independent of schemes, then everything is possible, since this decision comes to interfere with practical decisions (political and moral) and not only with theoretical observations. It certainly can be argued that ontology is not what there is, but it is the discourse on what there is. So there is always an epistemological remnant in ontology and an ontological residue in epistemology. This is indisputable: ontology is never without epistemology, just as one cannot live without knowledge. However, if onto*logy* is also a discourse, it is a discourse that must mark the difference with respect to epistemology and not insist on the continuity with it, as often happens favoring the fallacy of being-knowledge.[13] This is why, as trivial as it might be to confuse ontology and epistemology, the theoretically interesting maneuver cannot consist in saying that ontology and epistemology merge but precisely in emphasizing in which and how many ways ontology and epistemology are distinguished. I will try to summarize them in this scheme, and then I shall articulate them later in this chapter.

Epistemology	Ontology
Amendable What can be corrected	*Unamendable* What cannot be corrected
Internal World (= internal to conceptual schemes)	*External World* (= external to conceptual schemes)
Science Linguistic Historical Free Infinite Teleological	*Experience* Not necessarily linguistic Not historical Unamendable Finite Not necessarily teleological

AMENDABLE AND UNAMENDABLE

Let us come to the first essential distinction neglected by constructionists and by those who think that data are a myth: that between amendable and unamendable. I may or may not know that water is H_2O; I will get wet anyway, and I will not be able to dry up by means of the thought that hydrogen and oxygen as such are not wet. And this—in accordance with the slipper experiment—would also happen to a dog, with conceptual schemes different from mine, or to a worm, or even an inanimate being such as my computer (which, although unaware of the chemical composition of water, could undergo irreparable damage in the unfortunate case where a glass of water capsized on the keyboard).

As I said, I propose we define this fundamental character of reality's "unamendability": the fact that what we face cannot be corrected or changed by the mere use of conceptual schemes, unlike what happens in the hypothesis of constructivism. This, however, is not only a limit, it is also a resource.

Unamendability, in fact, informs us about the existence of an external world, not in relation to our body (which is part of the external world) but in relation to our minds and more specifically with respect to the conceptual schemes with which we try to explain and interpret the world. As we have seen (and we will return to this in chapter 3, when talking about "friction"), unamendability manifests itself primarily as a phenomenon of resistance and contrast. I can embrace all the theories of knowledge in this world, I can be atomistic or Berkeleyan, postmodernist or cognitivist, I can think, with naïve realism, that what is perceived is the true world, or I can think, with the Vedanta doctrine, that what is perceived is the false world. The fact remains that what we perceive is unamendable, it cannot be corrected: sunlight is blinding if the sun is up, and the handle of the coffee pot is hot if we leave it on the fire. There is no interpretation to be opposed to these facts: the only alternatives are sunglasses and potholders.

If the notion of reality as a "background" has been widely theorized by philosophers,[14] I would rather draw attention to a much less stressed aspect, namely, that this background is often at odds with our theories, that is, it does not constitute their obvious presupposition, since experience can be disharmonious or surprising. This point is more important than it may seem. Science is (following Aristotle) a way to grasp *regularities* and (empirically) *iterability* in experiments. A part of these features is found in experience, which, however, has to deal first of all with the *surprise*. Something unexpected can always happen and break the regularity. To what extent this condition can impact the image of science as a regularity was very well understood by empiricists, who, as we have said, found precisely in surprise and in the unexpectedness of experience an insuperable obstacle with respect to the reliability of induction. And yet if something new did not occasionally happen, something that breaks the series of our predictions, we would have no way to distinguish reality from imagination. But the surprise would be little useful if it could be immediately corrected. Now, one of the characteristics of experience is the fact that in many cases the surprise is there and cannot be corrected, there is nothing we can do, it is there and does not pass nor change. This characteristic is precisely unamendability, and it presents itself as a fundamental trait—as a persistent and nontransient character—of reality. The basic idea is essentially this: if we admit that a fundamental requirement of objectivity (also scientific) is invariance under transformation,[15] we must all the more assume that the independence of the object with respect to the subject's conceptual schemes (or epistemology in general) constitutes an even stronger criterion of objectivity. "Unamendability" is precisely this: looking at the fire, I can think that it is a phenomenon of oxidation or the action of phlogiston and caloric, but (unless I am provided with asbestos gloves) I cannot but burn myself if I put my hand in the fire. In short, unamendability is the sphere to which Wittgenstein refers in a famous passage of his: "If I have exhausted the justifications I have reached bedrock, and my spade is turned. Then I am inclined to say: 'this is simply what I do.'"[16] From this point of view, it is not surprising that a prominent manifestation of unamendability is exactly the framework of perception. From the ancient skeptics to Descartes, up to Hegel's *Phenomenology of Spirit*, the disregard of sensible experience took place according to a confusion between epistemology and ontology: the senses can be deceiving, *therefore* any authority, even ontological, of sensible experience, was denied. This, after all, would be like saying that since there may be sensible deceptions, then it is not possible to get burned in contact with fire—a circumstance that is actually evoked, ironically, in the refutation of skepticism proposed by Locke.[17] It is in view of these circumstances that I have given a peculiar ontological value to the recovery of aesthetics as a theory of sensibility,[18] developing the theory of unamendability closely with what Wolfgang Metzger and Gestalt psychology had elaborated under the category of "encountered reality," namely, the reality that gives itself while also contradicting our conceptual expectations,[19] thus antagonizing the "represented reality" dear to constructivists. This "encountered reality," in agreement with what Paolo Bozzi proposed under the category of "naïve physics,"[20] appears to be impermeable to knowledge and provides a patent case of a gap between knowledge of the world and experience of the world that helps one avoid the transcendental fallacy. Against a more or less openly constructionist perspective—from transcendentalism to the empiricist view of perception as an aggregation of "sense data"—unamendability, in fact, reveals how perceptive experience possesses an admirable stability and refractoriness compared to conceptual action and suggests that this stability should be ascribed more deeply (since, as in the slipper experiment, there is an interaction between beings with very different perceptual apparatuses) to the stability of the encountered world, prior to the action of our perceptual apparatuses and conceptual schemes, which I shall illustrate specifically by distinguishing between "internal world" and "external world."

Internal world and External World

In general, the "external world" is external to conceptual schemes, and, from this point of view, its paradigm lies in the unamendability of perception. However, we must not forget that there is a sphere of nonperceptive unamendables, as we shall see in the next chapter when talking about "irrevocability."[21] The case of perception, therefore, only constitutes an area of particular evidence, where unamendability can be found as 1) autonomy of aesthetics with respect to logic; 2) antinomy of aesthetics with respect to logic; 3) autonomy of the world with respect to our conceptual schemes and perceptive apparatuses.[22] Let us examine in detail these three points.

Autonomy of aesthetics with respect to logic. Let us return once again to the formulation of Descartes's condemnation of the senses: the senses deceive, and it is prudent never to rely on things that have once deceived us. Now, the senses have neither intentions nor character; if anything, they reveal a tendency to disappoint us, not to give us what we hoped for, and this is the opposite of the intention to deceive. Here we note the independence of perception from conceptual schemes or, in positive, the existence of nonconceptual contents. These contents manifest themselves precisely in the traditional discontent with perception, considered as a source of knowledge both necessary and unreliable.

Antinomy of aesthetics with respect to logic. If it were true that thought is constitutive of reality, unless we were masochists, not only would we see what we want but also and only what we like, and we would never be surprised. Instead, no matter what we do, we cannot help but see things we would rather not or could not see, or even things we have reason to believe do not exist or that are not as they appear, as indeed happens in optical illusions (which are called "illusions" only because we think that the eye is a support for science and truth). I can have all the philosophical beliefs of this world (or, which is more significant, I can be completely ignorant of philosophy), but the senses will continue to have it their way. From the perspective I propose, therefore, the appeal to sensibility turns out to be antithetical to sensism: whereas the sensist enhances the senses from the epistemological point of view, that is, as cognitive tools, I appreciate them from the ontological point of view, that is, precisely for the resistance they set against our conceptual schemes. It is from this antinomy that the autonomy of the world arises, that is, its transcendence with respect to thought.

Autonomy of the world with respect to our conceptual schemes and perceptive apparatuses. Reality possesses a structural (and structured) link that not only resists conceptual schemes and perceptive apparatuses (and unamendability consists of this resistance) but precedes them. For this reason, the concept of "external world" is to be understood primarily in the sense of "external to our conceptual schemes and perceptive apparatuses." Such a world exists; otherwise all our knowledge would be indistinguishable from a dream.[23] I can (and in certain circumstances I must) doubt the *veracity* of even all of my experiences but without doubting the fact that there is something in general.

Science and Experience

Third and final distinction. What the fallacy of being-knowledge does not consider is the crucial difference between experiencing something, talking about our experience, and doing science (for example, between having a headache, describing it to someone, and making a diagnosis). In the case of *talking* about an experience, and even more so in doing science, we are confronted with a *linguistic* activity (scientists talk) that is also historical (their activity is cumulative), free (one is able not to do science), infinite (science never ends), and teleological (it has a purpose). It is not so in the case of experience. Let us examine these elements, aware of the fact that it is precisely by neglecting the difference between science and experience that postmodernists have been able to argue that there is nothing outside the text, language, or some form of knowledge.

1. The importance of *language* and writing in science, as an inherently social fact, seems hardly contestable. There is no

doubt that scientificity has to do with documentality—which I shall discuss in chapter 3—namely, with a system of communication, inscription, acknowledgment, coding, filing, and patents. We can well imagine experiences that occur without language and without writing, conversely, to communicate the discoveries and to record them is a necessary condition for science: "publish or perish" is perhaps an academic aberration with regard to individual researchers, but it is a categorical imperative for science that, as a collective and progressive work, necessarily requires the communicative exchange (oral or written), the storage and the traditionalization of discoveries. None of this applies to experience, which can take place without any communication, recording, or need for linguistic rendering.

2. The intrinsic *historicity* of science is nothing but a corollary to the previous consideration. Science exists precisely insofar as each generation can capitalize on the discoveries made by previous generations. And it is for this reason that one can speak of relatively young sciences, indicating by this a biography, a growth, and a development, which derive precisely from the possibility of inscription and documentation. On the contrary, an expression like "young experience" appears completely meaningless or purely metaphorical: at most, we can have youthful experiences, that is, things that happen to us when we are young.

3. As for *freedom*, it is clear that science is a deliberate activity. At some point in the intellectual history of some civilizations, scientific activities began and then evolved freely, although in many cases responding to the pressure of practical needs. This genesis could also have not taken place: this is proved by the fact that other civilizations have not had a scientific development, while others have developed a science significantly different from ours. Here, again, the comparison with experience is illuminating, because experiences manifest

an intercultural constancy and do not appear as the result of a deliberate choice. I am not speaking only of perception, if we abandon the legends according to which the Inuit see more shades of white than we do. I am speaking of strongly structured elements, such as myths. In short, what is universal in humanity is not science (which is simply universalizable) but rather experience.

4. Coming to *infinity*, the most prestigious sciences are those that have a long history and a very long future ahead of them, namely, those that best respond to the idea of knowledge as infinite development. None of this can be said of experience, which not only is not designed as infinite (its period, in any case, cannot be longer than that of human life) but is not conceived as progressive either. This does not simply mean that the project to sharpen the senses faces objective limits (at most we can try to remedy their weakening with glasses or hearing aids), but that even in the area of common practices and techniques in life, progress is not necessarily an ideal. Everyone would surely prefer to be treated by a doctor of 2212 rather than by a doctor of 2012, and we would all dread the idea of resorting to a doctor of 1812, but the prospect of eating bread like it used to be or of getting our hands on a pre-globalization fabric may seem very tempting. Also, while the idea of the infinite progress of science is completely reasonable, thinking that there could be an infinite development of techniques such as how to tie one's shoes or one's tie is little more than a joke.

5. Finally, with regard to *teleology*, the point is very simple. Science is a deliberate activity, just like many techniques that, from this point of view, represent a middle way between science and experience: making the bed appears not to be an activity subject to an infinite progress (at most one can invent sheets with elastic gussets), but it is certainly a deliberate activity. This is even truer for science. If someone went to the laboratory for no reason, they would not be doing science, but someone

who, for no reason, felt heat, saw a color, or suffered from a toothache would have no reason to rule out the fact that they would be having those experiences. And although the history of science loves the serendipity of those who had fundamental insights in the bathtub or under an apple tree, when we move from folklore to assessments, intentionality, that is, teleological finality, counts and how. Typically, the discovery of penicillin by Fleming, which had a high degree of randomness (it was mold that accidentally developed in a refrigerator left open), appears as a less meritorious discovery than others, precisely because it is less deliberate.

POSITIVISM?

A final consideration. As I believe I have shown through the differences listed so far, the realism I propose is presented as antithetical to positivism. Yet, it happens sometimes that when we speak of "reality," some see in it an appeal to some form of scientism. Now, positivism is a theory dating back to two centuries ago, and when interpretation-friendly thinkers speak of the threat of positivism to express their impatience with facts, they remind one of the Italian populists that evoke the specter of communism even decades after the fall of the Wall. If, however, in my proposal of realism, I insist so much on the difference between ontology (what there is) and epistemology (what we know) it is because I completely reject this view. So, there is no "return to positivism." Rather, against positivism that enhances science and against postmodernism that boils it down to a struggle between interests (but at the same time brings it even into the most minute details of experience and nature), I propose a rebirth of philosophy as a bridge between the world of common sense, moral values, and opinions and the world of knowledge in general (because there is not only physics; there are also law, history, economics).

This is not at all to say that all truths are in the hands of science. In this case, philosophy would likely appear to be a parasitic knowledge exactly as in postmodern dreams: science does the real work, philosophers follow, as stewards, and either are silent or rattle. Now, the error made by postmodernists (and it is an error that comes from far away, think of Heidegger's claims on the fact that science does not think) was to want to build a knowledge alternative to science, a para- or super- or meta-science, or, more modestly but equally parasitically, a deconstructive knowledge with respect to science. In the end, however, the basic assumption was precisely that science is the only source of knowledge. However, the right question, which postmodernists rarely asked themselves, is: what are the areas in which science is really an instance of final appeal? Important pieces of nature, in a very advanced form in the case of the study of matter, in a rather advanced form in the case of the study of human physiology, and in a promising but embryonic form in the case of the study of the mind.

But if one scrolls through the pages of a newspaper, for example, one will realize that the percentage of problems on which science can say something is very low. The pages on politics, the comments, those on culture and economy are little enlightened by physics and medicine (the pages on sports are already better, because of doping). It is not science that we can turn to for the organization of that Library of Babel that is the Web or to satisfy the need that humans often have to examine their lives. Now, I am convinced that philosophy can give some answers, and that this is much easier if we leave aside the philosophical refrain of the last century: the superiority of the question over the answer, the fact that philosophy is structurally incapable of constructing something, that it does not have access to reality, and that indeed it is the doctrine whose mission consists in saying that the real world does not exist. In short, bridging knowledge and beliefs is not a cushy job. For this, however, a reconstructive philosophy is required. In the next chapter I would like to suggest some proposals in this direction.

THREE

RECONSTRUCTION

Why Criticism Starts from Reality

The Fallacy of Ascertainment-Acceptance

Recall the objection according to which the only purpose of realism is to affirm the existence of reality. An ethical-political variant of it lies in claiming that realism implies the acceptance of the existing state of things (which is to say that ontology accepts reality and oncology accepts tumors). But of course it is not so: realism, as I propose it, is a *critical* doctrine in two ways: in the Kantian sense of judging what is real and what is not, and in the Marxian sense of transforming what is not right. That this dual dimension may not seem obvious to some depends precisely on what I suggest we call the "fallacy of ascertainment-acceptance," that is, the dogma for which ascertaining reality is equated to accepting it. Just like Chance, the gardener of *Being There*, tries to get rid of what he has in front of him by fiddling with a TV remote control, the postmodernist believes that it is enough to say that *everything* is socially constructed to immunize himself from the friction of reality. As such, the fallacy of ascertainment-acceptance is a direct consequence of the fallacy of being-knowledge. The world is my construction: can I not change it whenever I want? Or maybe it is a construction of others: a further reason to decree its unreality. But this is a perspective that is hard not only to share but also to understand. Think of doctors: they want to learn about diseases certainly not so as to accept them but to treat them. Conversely, Chance's strategy involves an extreme quietism: if it rains, we can say that rain is socially constructed, but our profession of faith will not make the rain stop. It will thus reveal itself for what it is: a vain complaint like that of "it's raining, damn the government!"[1] One cannot break free from reality (assuming it makes sense to break free from reality instead of pursuing a critical action over it) with a mere act of skepticism, precisely because being is independent of knowledge. Reciprocally, realism is the first step on the path of criticism and emancipation (or at least of nonmystification).

Those who do not accept the unamendability of reality do not accept it—understandably—in order to escape from frustrations ranging from the relatively trivial loss of objects to the shame for the sins committed, up to extreme forms of unamendability—as when, in the *Recherche*, Françoise announces to the Narrator that "Mademoiselle Albertine has gone," or when in *War and Peace* the princesses who witnessed Bolkonsky's death wonder "Where has he gone? Where is he now?" But precisely in this unamendability lies the foundation of morality. Derrida has claimed that justice is the undeconstructable,[2] meaning by this that the desire for justice underlies deconstruction itself and cannot in turn be subjected to deconstruction. I would suggest that justice is the undeconstructable not because it has nothing to do with ontology, but precisely because ontology is the unamendable. Precisely because there is a real world whose laws are indifferent to our volitions and cogitations it is possible that, in such a world, there is science and there is justice. Criticism is therefore incorporated in realism, while acquiescence is inherent to antirealism—which, from the prisoners of Plato's cave, brings us up to the illusions of the postmodernists. Thus, the decisive argument for realism is not theoretical but moral, because it is not possible to imagine moral behavior in a world without facts and without objects.

EXPERIMENT OF THE ETHICAL BRAIN

This can be better understood with a thought experiment that is an ethical version of the *Gedankenexperiment* of the brain in a vat.[3] The idea is this: imagine that a mad scientist has put some brains in a vat and is feeding them artificially. By means of electrical stimulation, these brains have the impression of living in a real world, but in fact what they feel is the result of simple electrical stimulations. Imagine that those stimulations depict situations that require moral stances: some snitch and some sacrifice themselves for freedom, some commit embezzlement, and some commit acts of holiness. Can we really say that in those circumstances there are moral acts?

In my opinion, we cannot: these are, in the best-case scenario, representations with moral content, but they do not take place in the outside world—so much so that they can be amended at will, for example, through other stimulations. Here we can test the validity of the saying according to which you cannot judge someone on mere intent: imposing a prison sentence on a brain that thought—or rather, that in this case *was made to think*—of stealing, is no less unjust (or more exactly, nonsensical) than sanctifying a brain that has thought about making holy actions. This experiment simply shows that thought alone is not enough for there to be morals, and that the latter begins when there is an external world that provokes us and allows us to perform actions, and not simply to imagine them.

So, instead of imposing on us how we should act (this, hopefully, is suggested to us by our consciousness), ontology tells us that there is a world in which our actions are real and not mere dreams or imaginations. Through the appeal to the distinction between ontology and epistemology proposed in chapter 2, I therefore declare myself a supporter of a modest or minimalist realism for which ontology serves as an opposition, as a limit.[4] This obviously has nothing to do with the appeal to some law of nature. And in this respect, we might ask ourselves whether natural rights (which are mostly natural duties) are not a joke invented to allow one to write postmodern books on the fact that nature does not exist. It is obvious that from nature one cannot obtain any rights or duties. However, the fact remains that nature exists, involving constraints (for example, the duration of life or the laws of physics), and these constraints are not constructed by people. In short, there is an essential difference between the laws on pensions and the laws of thermodynamics, which in fact are never called into question by even the most reckless financial acts. In this framework "living according to nature" means "do not throw yourself off the plane without a parachute, because you do not have wings" and not "the heterosexual family is ordained by nature and is the basis of society." Far from yearning for a law of nature, it is, therefore, a matter of starting from what I call the "friction of reality":[5] an ethical version of unamendability echoing Kant's observation that in the absence of the resistance of air even the dove, moral symbol of absoluteness, could not fly. Even in more radically idealistic systems, like that proposed by Fichte, the presence of a real independent of the subject (and therefore marking the difference between what exists and what is merely thought of) is offered by a backlash, by the action of a non-I who is opposed to the I. For this reason unamendability as a fundamental ontological character is central, precisely to the extent that it is not a normative order (as claimed by its enemies, who consider the appeal to ontology as a submission to the law of nature, or even to human arrogance) but simply a line of resistance against falsifications and denials.

"Very-Differentism" and Irrevocability

To the ethical brain experiment and the friction of the real, antirealists could reply with an argumentative move dear to them, the very-differentism, which consists in claiming that we may all agree on the (trivial) existence of tables and chairs, but that philosophically important things are "very different." But is it really so? Primo Levi wrote of the "shame the Germans did not know, that the just man experiences at another man's crime; the feeling of guilt that such a crime should exist, that it should have been introduced irrevocably into the world of things that exist, and that his will for good should have proved too weak or null, and should not have availed in defence."[6] In chapter 2, I spoke about "unamendability," which is manifested with particular clarity in the sphere of perceptive experience: I have no way to correct an optical illusion, although I am aware of its illusory nature, and the same goes for heat, weight, or the dimensions of a body. However, the sphere of unamendability does not simply concern the area of perception and is rather manifested, in a macroscopic form, in the irrevocability of past events.

Take for example the case of dinosaurs: they existed millions of years ago; then they disappeared and fossils remain of them. This is clear evidence of the fact that there can be whole forms of organized life that develop fully independently of our language, our knowledge, and our conceptual schemes.[7] It is also, if you will, the manifestation of an ontology that existed millions of years before any possible epistemology. Now, even in areas that depend on conceptual schemes, such as historical events, we deal with a clear manifestation of unamendability, which is the irrevocability of past events on which historians construct their interpretations.[8] For example, it is a fact that in 1813, in Leipzig, the Saxons abandoned Napoleon and sided with the Austrians, Prussians, Russians, and Swedes; it is an event that can be assessed in different ways, but it is a fact, and someone who claimed that it did not take place would not give a better interpretation of what happened but would merely say something false. Acknowledging the fact that there have been dinosaurs and that in Leipzig the Saxons changed alliances can hardly be considered an uncritical attitude toward the real. It is a neutral attitude, which has to be assumed in any criticism. The question of whether the Saxons have done well or not in changing alliances, for example, is a legitimate question, but you can only ask it insofar as the Saxons did actually change alliances.

Claiming (as the very-differentists do) that there is a gap between perceptions and facts, and then between facts and judgments, would perhaps be possible—however, only if one were able to indicate the point of discontinuity in which one passes from the unamendable and irrevocable to the interpretable. Now, it is precisely this discontinuity that seems unobtainable: assessments are made on facts and facts take place in a world of objects. If this is so, it is not true that the ascertainment of facts in the physical world (for instance, that snow is white)[9] lies at a radically distinct level from the ascertainment of facts in the historical world and, in general, in a higher sphere where, according to the very-differentists, the decisive matches are played and interpretations have emancipative functions. There is an unbroken thread that leads from the fact that snow is white if and only if snow is white to the fact that, in the same snow, on January 27, 1945, the soldiers of the Red

Army entered Auschwitz and saw the "shame the Germans did not know." Sure, you may *decide* to introduce a discontinuity, but the price would be very high, because if you cut at any point the wire that leads from the snow to the Holocaust, then any denial becomes possible. If this is the case, the "very different" something appealed to by those who argue that tables and chairs are devoid of philosophical relevance is connected to the world of tables and chairs by a robust and continuous wire, which cannot be broken—otherwise one will fall into meaninglessness or irresponsibility.

Deconstruction

Therefore, the point is not to claim that there is a discontinuity between facts and interpretations but rather to understand what objects are constructed and what are not, by means of a process of deconstruction opposite to the all-encompassing thesis that everything is socially constructed. On this point we should make a preliminary consideration. A decade ago the historian of science Ian Hacking proposed, at the beginning of his book,[10] a list of objects that, according to postmodernists, are socially constructed: the notion of "authorship," that of "brotherhood," the child viewer of television, danger, emotions, facts, gender, homosexual culture, illness, knowledge, literacy, the medicalized immigrant, nature, oral history, postmodernism, quarks, reality, serial homicides, technological systems, urban schooling, vital statistics, women refugees, youth homelessness, Zulu nationalism, mind, panic, the eighties. And he added that, during a workshop on underage motherhood, a Catholic agent declared: "and, obviously, I am a social construction *myself*; we all are." Apart from the vaguely comic and vertiginous effect à la Borges's encyclopedia, the feeling we get is that of a mess. In fact, it is difficult to doubt that the notion of copyright is socially constructed, just as it is indisputable that there are whole categories, for example, that of "Orientalism," object of an admirable analysis by Edward Said,[11] that are not only constructed but inconsistent. But is it the same for reality or nature? And is it really critical and deconstructive to formulate such massive theses on reality?

In my opinion, no. Stating that everything is socially constructed and that there are no facts, only interpretations, is not deconstructing but, on the contrary, means formulating a thesis—the more accommodating in reality the more it is critical in imagination—that leaves everything as it is. There is indeed a great conceptual work that interpretation-friendly thinkers withdraw from when they say that everything is socially constructed—which, *nota bene*, implies that tables and chairs do not have a separate existence, that is, to put it more bluntly, that they do not really exist in the mode of existence that common sense usually attributes to tables and chairs.

This work consists in distinguishing carefully between the existence of things that exist only for us, that is, things that only exist if there is a humanity, and things that would exist even if humanity had never been there. That is why, in my opinion, the real deconstruction must commit to distinguishing between regions of being that are socially constructed and others that are not, to establishing for each region of being some specific modes of existence, and finally to ascribing individual objects to one of these regions of being, proceeding case by case.[12]

In order to respond to this need, elsewhere[13] I proposed to divide objects into three classes: *natural objects* that exist in space and time independently of subjects, *social objects* that exist in space and time dependently on subjects, and *ideal objects* that exist outside of space and time independently of subjects. It is at this point that controversies can begin. Recall the three differences that derived from the distinction between ontology and epistemology that I presented in chapter 2. They aimed at demonstrating what the fundamental misunderstanding of constructivism was: the belief that reality has no form without the action of a conceptual construction and that data are a myth. But at this point, of course, a commonsensical objection arises: are you trying to deny that VAT is socially constructed? Or worse, do you believe that VAT is unamendable in the relevant fora? Of course not. The distinctions I have proposed are designed precisely to avoid the two complementary absurdities of saying that there is nothing socially constructed, not even VAT, or that everything is socially constructed, including tuberculosis. This is because the target of the realist is constructionism, not some kind of Berkeleyan idealism. In fact, no realist would deny that VAT depends on conceptual schemes (which still does not mean to claim that they are purely subjective: VAT is applied—in principle—to all those who shop in the United States). What the realist asks is how far the action of conceptual schemes gets, and it is here that the conflict between realists and postmodernists manifests itself. The latter are much more generous in the list of parts of reality they deem socially constructed, to the point of saying, in extreme cases, that we do not ever have access to a world "out there," and that what we come in contact with is constructed by our conceptual schemes.

That is why the distinction is especially critical between social objects and natural objects. The first, in fact, unlike the latter, *constitutively* undergo the action of epistemology because things like marriages or debts exist only insofar as there are people who know that they exist. There is an essential difference between being ill and not knowing it (we do not know it, but the disease runs its course) and being married and not knowing it (we do not know it and, if others do not know it either, it is just as if we were not). Consider, therefore, these two statements: 1) "Mountains, lakes, beavers, and asteroids depend on our conceptual schemes"; 2) "Banknotes, qualifications, debts, rewards, and punishments depend on our conceptual schemes."

It takes a lot of courage to argue that mountains and rivers are what they are because there are people whose senses work in a certain way and because there are categories of a certain type. In fact, mountains and rivers are what they are on their own; if anything, they are *known* by us through the specific forms of our senses and our intellect. But now let us look at social objects.

Here we could really say that marriages and divorces, mortgages and chess games, debts and parliament seats, years in prison and Nobel prizes are so and so because our senses and our intellect are made in a certain way. It is an unsurprising thesis. For a beaver—we can have reasonable certainty of this—mortgages and divorces do not exist, while mountains and lakes certainly exist. Once we recognize and explain the distinction between ontology and epistemology, as well as between the classes of objects, the way is open for a rehabilitation of the Kantian insight into a different sphere from that in which it was born, that is no longer in reference to natural objects but indeed in relation to social objects. The basic idea is that a thesis like "intuitions without concepts are blind," which we recognized as difficult to apply to the natural world, explains very well our relationship with the social world, which is made up of objects such as money, roles, institutions that exist only because we believe they exist.

So, *I do not at all mean to argue that there are no interpretations in the social world.* Of course there are interpretations, and of course deconstructions are needed. But the most important thing, for philosophers and non-philosophers, is not to confuse natural objects (such as Mont Blanc or a hurricane, which are there whether there are people and their interpretations or not) with social objects such as promises, bets, and marriages, which only exist if there are people equipped with certain conceptual schemes. If by hypothesis a believer, an agnostic, and the Indian of Mato Grosso photographed a few years ago, who belongs to a tribe that has remained Neolithic, were in front of the Shroud, they would all see the same natural object; then the believer would think that he is seeing the shroud of Christ and the agnostic would regard it as a sheet of medieval origin. Yet, they would see the *same* physical object as that seen by the Indian, who has no notion of our cultural world. In the social world, then, what we know counts indeed, that is, epistemology is determining in relation to ontology: what we think, what we say, our interactions are crucial, and it is crucial that these interactions are recorded and documented. This is why the social world is full of documents, in archives, in our drawers, in our wallets, and now even in our mobile phones.

CRITICISM

To indicate the paradigm of the political commitment of a philosopher, people always quote Marx's eleventh thesis on Feuerbach: "The philosophers have only *interpreted* the world, in various ways: the point, however, is to *change* it." What people forget to mention is the first thesis: "Feuerbach wants sensuous objects, really distinct from the thought objects, *but* he does not conceive human activity itself as *objective* activity." Now, in my proposal, the constitutive law of social objects is *Object = Inscribed Act*. That is to say that a social object is the result of a social act (such as to involve at least two people, or a delegated machine and a person) that is characterized by being recorded, on a piece of paper, on a computer file, or even only in the mind of the people involved in the act. What I propose under the title of "documentality" is thus a "weak textualism" (that is, also a "weak constructionism"): weak because it assumes that inscriptions are decisive in the construction of *social* reality, but—contrary to what we may define "strong textualism," practiced by postmodernists—it excludes that inscriptions may be constitutive of reality *in general*. Weak textualism is therefore such since it results from the weakening of Derrida's thesis that "there is nothing outside the text," which is transformed into "there is nothing *social* outside the text."[14] It admits a kind of constructionism but, indeed, a moderate constructionism, which does not clash with the realistic intuition. In addition to recognizing a positive ontological sphere, this move allows us to avoid the inconsistencies that derive from the lack of distinction between objects and from the collapse between ontology and epistemology, saving us a lot of "fashionable nonsense."

But, above all, the reference to social objects has an inherently critical value. Postmodernists not only argued that nature is socially constructed, a thesis that has more or less the effect of a joke. More seriously, they have supported a form of irrealism of social objects, which is what lies at the basis of the argument that postmodernity is a liquid and evanescent reality. Through the analysis of the specific characteristics of social objects, it emerges instead that society is anything but liquid: it is made of objects such as promises and bets, money and passports, which can often be more solid than tables and chairs, and which all the happiness and unhappiness of our lives depend on. Unfortunately, those who have variable-rate mortgages or lost their savings on the stock market know this very well. The illusion that these objects are an infinitely interpretable phantasmagoria makes us blind, and therefore helpless, in front of the world in which we live. So I formulated a definition of social objects as "inscriptions of acts," that is, as the establishment of relationships that access the dimension of objectivity through recording.

Now, next to the positive side of the construction of a class of objects, we also have the revelation of the fallacy of the link between derealization and emancipation that was formed by postmodernism. This link would find its typical representation in the Web: the world where we are all given back our time, working where we want and when we want, and social networks take us away from loneliness and subrogate the old forms of social organization. And yet it is not so, in two senses. First of all, it is not true that, from the political and ideological point of view, all this fluidity is emancipation. As we saw in chapter 1, all the promised emancipation in postmodernism has turned into a form of subordination (often voluntary, but this is not the point).

Also, and this time from an ontological perspective, (that is what exists independently of what we think or hope), liquid postmodernity showed another face, which is not that of a floating world but rather that of a total mobilization. Jünger's idea of the militarized worker[15] is realized, in an unexpected form, and it is realized not in the world of storms of steel and factories but in that of silicon and mobile phones—the same mobile phones that give us the impression that we have the world in our hands while we are in the hands of the world, always available for its impositions and demands. If this mobilization is possible, it is because of the fundamental nature of new technologies, namely, recording and inscription: the fact that in every moment, every act and every said thing can be fixated and count as an obligation, demand, blackmail, responsibility.[16] In this case, recognizing recording and inscription as a characteristic proper of social objects allows precisely for that critical realism that was impossible to postmodernism, which saw, wrongly, the new world as a soft fairy tale and a lightening process. Far from being fluid, modernity is the era in which words are stones and in which the nightmare of *verba manent* is realized. Thus, from the ontological point of view, we have a multiplication of social objects, and then, exactly to the opposite of what postmodernists thought, an increase of *realia* rather than a derealization.

RECONSTRUCTION

Beyond the analyses and the criticism, the distinctions proposed here allow for a reconstruction[17] that the nucleus of positive realism consists of. I shall try to summarize its fundamental steps. First, as regards the distinction between ontology and epistemology (and the distinctions that follow, between external world and internal world, and between science and experience), it seems to me that it responds to the necessity to preserve two essential needs for realism, so as to overcome the fallacy of being-knowledge, that is, the collapse between objects and the knowledge we have of them that began with transcendental philosophy and culminated with postmodernism. On the one hand, we should stick to the fact that there is an unamendable core of being and experience that gives itself in complete independence from conceptual schemes and knowledge. On the other hand, we must leave open the possibility of constructing, upon this layer, knowledge as a conceptual, linguistic, deliberate, and above all emancipative activity. If, instead, we saw knowledge as a simple game of conceptual schemes that are all equivalent as per their truth content, we should resign ourselves to considering science not as a search for truth (with the emancipation that goes with it) but as a conflict between different wills to power—which is actually what is alleged by the fallacy of knowledge-power on which I will focus in the next chapter.

Second, as to the distinction between natural objects and social objects, it seems to be a decisive element to circumvent the fallacy of ascertainment-acceptance and to make social reality into a concrete ground of analysis and transformation. On the one hand, in fact, it allows us to recognize the natural world as independent of human construction, avoiding the nihilistic and skeptical outcome that is reached when trying to dialectize the distinction between nature and culture. On the other hand, it allows us to see in the social world the work of human construction, which however—precisely to the extent to which it is a social interaction—does not constitute a purely subjective production. In this way, the sphere of natural objects, as well as that of social objects, becomes the field of a possible and legitimate knowledge, that is, of an epistemology that undoubtedly involves hermeneutics (since in many cases knowledge requires varying degrees of interpretation). Nevertheless, this epistemology has a very different value depending on whether it refers to natural objects or social objects. In respect of the former, in fact, epistemology exerts a purely reconstructive function, merely acknowledging something that exists independently of knowledge. In respect of social objects, however, epistemology has a constitutive value, both in the sense that a certain amount of knowledge is necessary to live in any social world and in the sense in which it is obvious that in the social world new objects are produced (for example, through legislative activity) with an operation that is not purely of acknowledgment (as is the reference to natural objects) but is performative.

Turning now to the choice of the constitutive rule Object = Inscribed Act, it arises from the need to provide an alternative to the constitutive rule proposed by the most influential theorist of social objects, John Searle, that is, the rule "X counts as Y in C" (the physical object X counts as the social object Y in a context C). The limit of this proposal is twofold. On the one hand, it does not seem able to account for complex social objects such as businesses, or negative entities such as debts, in which at first it seems difficult to find a physical object to be turned into a social object. On the other hand, it makes the entire social reality depend on the action of a rather mysterious entity, that is, collective intentionality, which allegedly manages the transformation of the physical into the social.[18] According to the version I propose, on the contrary, it is very easy to account for the totality of social objects, from informal promises to the corporate architectures of businesses, to negative entities such as, indeed, debts. In all these cases there is a minimal structure, which is guaranteed by the presence of at least two people who commit an act (which may consist of a gesture, a word, or writing) that can be recorded on some support, even if it were only human memory. In addition to accounting for the physical basis of the social object—which is not an X generally available for the action of collective intentionality but a recording that can take place on multiple supports—the rule I propose (and that I call the "rule of documentality" as opposed to the "rule of intentionality" with which we could designate Searle's option) has the advantage of not making social reality depend on a function, that is, collective intentionality. This notion, in fact, is dangerously close to a purely mental process and led Searle to make an affirmation that was anything but realistic: namely, that the economic crisis is largely the result of imagination.[19] Being a form of documentality, money is far from imaginary, and this very circumstance allows us to draw a distinction between the social (which records the acts of at least two people, even if the recording takes place in people's minds and not on external documents) and the mental (which can take place even only in the mind of a single individual). In this sense, the argument against Searle (who, in defining money as a result of imagination, acts like a postmodernist) comes from the elaboration of Derrida's theory on the role of writing in the construction of social reality. In short, once we circumscribe, as I proposed, the "there is nothing outside the text" to a more limited "there is nothing social outside the text," there is a good argument—I believe—to counter Searle's thesis on collective intentionality—which in hindsight sounds like a "there is nothing social outside the mind," making the distinction between social objects and mental objects collapse.

There remains one last point, which concerns precisely the mental. One may legitimately wonder what the origin of documentality is, that is, where the intentions that underlie the inscriptions constituting social reality come from. Postmodern thinkers much insisted on the fact that the subject is not to be regarded as a fundamental datum, but their position, usually, did not go much beyond the criticism of a chosen target—the "Cartesian subject"—and the mere hypothesis that the subject is influenced by culture. The prospect of documentality, in my opinion, allows instead for a positive development, which begins with the theory that—from the ancients to the moderns—conceives the mind as a *tabula* on which inscriptions are imprinted. In fact, as we have seen, inscriptions have a powerful action in social reality: social behaviors are determined by laws, rituals, norms, and social structures, and education forms our intentions. Imagine some Crusoe figure who was the first and last man on the face of the earth. Could he ever be eaten away by the ambition to become an admiral, a billionaire, or a court poet? Certainly not, just like he could not sensibly aspire to follow fashions, or to collect baseball cards, or still lives. And if, say, he tried to fabricate a document, he would be undertaking an impossible task, because to make a document there must be at least two people, the writer and the reader. In fact, our arch Robinson would not even have a language, and one could hardly say that he would "think" in the usual sense of the term. And it would seem difficult to argue that he was proud, arrogant, or in love, for roughly the same reason why it would be absurd to claim he had friends or enemies.

We thus have two circumstances that reveal the social structure of the mind.[20] On the one hand, the mind cannot arise unless it is immersed in a social bath, made up of education, language, transmission, and recording of behaviors. On the other hand, there is the huge category of social objects that could not exist if there were not people who think that they exist. Instead of portraying a world at the total disposal of the subject, the sphere of social objects reveals the inconsistency of solipsism: the fact that in the world there are also others in addition to us is proven precisely by the existence of these objects, which would not serve any purpose in a world where there was only one subject. If it was not possible to keep traces, there would be no mind, and it is not by chance that the mind was traditionally depicted as a *tabula rasa*, a surface on which impressions and thoughts are inscribed. But without the possibility of inscription, there would not even be social objects, which consist in the recording of social acts, starting from the fundamental one of the promise. And, if this is the case, perhaps we should translate Aristotle's sentence that man is a *zoon logon echon* as: man is an animal endowed with inscriptions, or rather (since one of the meanings of *logos* in Greek is precisely "promise," "given word") as "man is an animal that promises."[21]

In analyses I recently carried out,[22] I propose, therefore, to see intentionality (as the hallmark of the mental) as a result of documentality. The mental, in accordance with the picture of the mind as a *tabula*, is a surface for inscriptions (which in terms of contemporary neurophysiology correspond to neuronal discharges). These inscriptions are not forms of thought nor do they require thought, just as computer operations do not require knowledge of arithmetic. And yet the result of inscriptions, progressing in complexity, is thought, just as the result of computer operations is an arithmetical calculation. Both in artificial intelligence and in the natural one the same process occurs, for which organization precedes and produces understanding,[23] and documentality precedes and produces intentionality.

The result of the reconstruction I propose is, as announced in chapter 2, a "treaty of perpetual peace" between the realist insight and the constructionist one. It is simply a matter of assigning each one to its field of competence: 1) Natural objects are independent of epistemology and make natural science true. 2) Experience is independent of science. 3) Social objects are dependent on epistemology, without being subjective. 4) "Intuitions without concepts are blind" applies primarily to social objects (where it has a constructive value) and less to the epistemological approach to the natural world (where it has a reconstructive value). 5) The realist intuition and the constructionist insight have therefore equal legitimacy in their respective fields of application. We can obviously dispute on questions such as: Are there subatomic entities? What kind of existence do promises have? Are species and genders a part of nature or culture? This is the real debate, and it is here that the philosophical, political, and scientific discussion takes place. Conversely, the best way to nip all dialogue and comparison in the bud is that of embracing pan-constructionism, because of an implacable law of politics that, incidentally, shows that even in the field of human things we deal with admirable regularities.

FOUR

EMANCIPATION

Unexamined Life Has No Value

The Fallacy of Knowledge-Power

All that is left now is the third fallacy, that of knowledge-power: that is, the main argument through which postmodernism committed to knock Enlightenment out. If Enlightenment linked knowledge to emancipation, in postmodernism the Nietzschean view prevailed according to which knowledge is an instrument of domination and a manifestation of the will to power. At this point, the only critical knowledge is a form of counterpower that is committed to systematically doubting knowledge itself, exercising a deconstruction without reconstruction—something that, besides, is consistent with the assumption that philosophy has no autonomous cognitive value. This fallacy has its origin in a philosophical critique of science that comes, paradoxically, from an almost superstitious overestimation of it on the part of its critics. I say "critics" and not "supporters" because it is especially the first that developed the idea (which, as we saw in chapter 2, has no *raison d'être*) that there is a science for everything, and that everywhere science undermines philosophy, which thus loses any constructive value and gathers in the foyer of criticism. Hence, with an accusation of co-responsibility, the insistence on the idea that, just like the *belles lettres*, science also makes use of words, words, words and is never in direct contact with the world "out there." The treatment given to science is also applied to metaphysics, suspected of conniving with science at the level of truth and reality; to the point that the overcoming of metaphysics has become the partisan struggle of those who had amnestied Heidegger's Nazism.

A first version of knowledge-power is that which, by radicalizing the connection between knowledge and interest, simply aims at calling into question the idea that there are disinterested reasons at the basis of knowledge. This weak form cannot even be properly defined a fallacy, as it recognizes something true. Undoubtedly, knowledge can be animated by the will to power or, in a completely trivial sense, by career interests. From this, however, it does not follow that we should doubt the results of knowledge, because even if it were true that (as Rousseau suggested)[1] astronomy was born out of superstition; eloquence out of ambition, hatred, or flattery; geometry out of greed; physics out of a vain curiosity; and morals itself out of pride, there would still be no reason to doubt the fact that the earth revolves around the sun, or that the sum of the interior angles of a triangle is 180 degrees. Strictly speaking, therefore, here we are not dealing with a fallacy but merely with a rule of prudence that does not prevent us from holding on to the Enlightenment idea of knowledge as emancipation.[2]

A second, more classical, version of the fallacy comes from Foucault's analyses and is consubstantial with the genesis of the first part of his thought.[3] The basic idea is that the organization of knowledge is strictly determined by motives of power:

it is not a mere statement of fact that determined that madness should cease to have a relationship with divine inspiration and be delivered to the sphere of pathology;[4] the fractures that caused changes in knowledge about man in modern times meet power's needs.[5] Inversely, the organizations of power are always able to develop knowledge, to the point that even the prison structure, which should be the least interested in knowledge, may manifest an ideal of control, which is represented in the emblematic form of the Panopticon designed by Bentham, that is, an apparatus that allows for total control over the prisoners.[6] Also in this case, the theory had a *raison d'être* and yet came to unlikely outcomes. Of course madness was segregated, but should the antipsychiatric movement be considered as a manifestation of the will to power as well? And what about the struggles by Foucault himself in favor of prisoners? Will to power even in that case? And when the Church acknowledged that Galileo was right, was it a manifestation of power or truth? But even apart from these aporias, the greatest weakness of this thesis revealed itself in the mechanical and monotone applications of the equivalence between knowledge and power that turned into an antiscientific and superstitious dogma.[7]

Then we have a third version of the fallacy of knowledge-power, an amplified one, wherein lies the basis of the ideal of a "weak thought." Here the argument of knowledge-power sounds like this: those who think they possess the truth tend to be dogmatic or even violent. It is a problematic thesis, because it does not account for at least three circumstances: first, that it is a matter of understanding what is meant by "truth," if that of the possessed mystical or that of the reasonable scholar (and therefore hardly violent, by the virtue of her doctrine and rationality); second, that you can have truth without violence and violence without truth, and that consequently the abandonment of truth does not lead to the abandonment of violence and universal peace but only to superstition; third, that, just as in "there are no facts, only interpretations," one can always hold against weak thought the argument that, if the explanation of the link between violence and truth is a truth, then weak thought is guilty of the same violence it condemns. Retaliations aside, there remain some considerations of common sense. The right response to those who manifest a wish to kill in the name of truth would not lie in attacking truth and pointing the finger at its social dangers, but, if anything, in observing that certainties not grounded in facts can have disastrous results—which is not at all an argument against truth but, on the contrary, the strongest argument in favor of truth and reality. If someone fights against the windmills, the best thing is to make him see the truth, namely, that they are windmills and not giants spinning their arms. Finally, everyday there is the case of someone (for example, an anti-Mafia magistrate) who fights for the truth, and such truth is objectively true. The objections that weak thought makes to truth as violence are, even under cursory examination, objections to violence, not to truth, and are therefore based on a misunderstanding. Omitting these circumstances leads us to situations without a way out: power is always right, or, conversely, counterpower is always wrong; and even, in a rather perverse form, counterpower and counterknowledge—even if they were proposed by criminals or by witches—are always right.

EXPERIMENT OF THE FAREWELL TO TRUTH

Finally, there is an extreme outcome, which consists in *considering truth as such as negative* and in an appeal to say goodbye to truth.[8] This outcome is so paradoxical that it lends itself to a thought experiment against the fallacy of knowledge-power, that is, to try to put into practice the farewell to truth. Here are some propositions that would become possible after this farewell: "The sun revolves around the earth", "2 + 2 = 5"; "Foucault is the author of *The Betrothed*," "Naomi's dad was Craxi's driver." And, passing from farce to tragedy: "The Holocaust is an invention of the Jews." Since these sentences follow quite naturally from the acceptance of the argument that there are no facts, only interpretations—of which the farewell to truth is the nihilistic extreme—we wonder how it is possible that someone might calmly assert that to claim that snow is white if and only if snow is white is a triviality unworthy of discussion. A banality that, at the same time, would not entail any consequence from the ethical, political, and human solidarity standpoint, that is, from the point of view dear to interpretation-friendly thinkers. No, there are consequences indeed. Not only—as we saw in chapter 3 when talking about very-differentism and irrevocability—is there an uninterrupted path leading from perception to morals, but this path can also be taken in the other direction: a little bit like what happens to Bouvard and Pécuchet, who, after pointing out discrepancies in the dates of the Olympics and the birth of Christ, come to the point of disdaining facts and conclude that the only important thing is the philosophy of history. What in them is farce can always result in tragedy, following the slippery slope that leads from the criticism of knowledge to skepticism and hence to negationism.

There is still a point to consider, passing from the extremism of the farewell to truth to more temperate and less nihilistic versions. Rorty's idea that truth is of no use and that it is maybe a beautiful but useless thing, being a sort of compliment or pat on the shoulder,[9] was the reversal of a no less objectionable idea proposed by William James, according to whom true propositions are those that enhance life. In both cases the arguments were set out with the best intentions, but if James's one could be seductive though false, Rorty's seemed problematic even under superficial examination, since it did not consider how important truth is in our daily practices, and how truth is intimately connected with reality. After all, it is not useless to know if the mushroom we are about to eat is poisonous, and this does not depend on our discursive practices or on our theories about mushrooms but on the mushroom. Now, let's say that, by applying the theory of the irrelevance of truth, I eat a poisonous mushroom. The first thing I would feel the need of is a doctor: not a supportive doctor but an objective doctor, one that would be able, if possible, to cure me. And if the poisoning proved to be beyond remedy (with mushrooms, it is unfortunate but true—it can happen) then I would perhaps be happy to have a supportive doctor, but it does not seem appropriate to mistake the fallback for the ideal.

In short, the farewell to reality and truth is not a painless event. The thesis of truth as an "effect of power" does not seem to consider the fact that it had already been represented in common sense, millennia before postmodernism, by the fable of the wolf and the lamb; the thesis of the primacy of solidarity over objectivity does not seem to take into account that solidarity can be what keeps a criminal association together, or worse. In fact, we cannot ignore, for example, the strong evidence that the primacy of people's solidarity against the objectivity of facts was the guiding principle of the Nazi courts after the attack on Hitler on July 20, 1944—and in general the Nazi regime is the glaring example of a society characterized by a strong internal solidarity, which remitted the management of truth to the care of Dr. Goebbels. In short, those who enounce the theory of the superiority of solidarity over objectivity—which is summed up in a paradoxical "Amica veritas magis amicus Plato," that is, a principle of authority—neglect the fact that this superiority can be used (as in fact happened) for the worst harassments and falsifications. Is the activity of so-called "Manufacturing Consent," for example, not a manufacturing of solidarity? One could conclusively note that there is no will to power more violent than that which comes from the acceptance of the fallacy of knowledge-power. Consider the two fundamental equations of postmodernism: 1) being = knowledge and 2) knowledge = power. For the transitive property we have: being = knowledge = power, and therefore: being = power.[10] In fact, the most extreme postmodernism brings about the logical step for which the combination of constructivism (reality is constructed by knowledge) and nihilism (knowledge is constructed by power) makes reality into a construction of power, which makes it both detestable (if by "power" one means the Moloch that dominates us) and malleable (if by "power" one means: "in our power"). This final outcome of postmodernism, which reduces being to power, recalls the destruction of reason: namely, the delegitimization of Enlightenment that Lukács[11] recognized as the essence of the arch that, starting from Romanticism and the late Schelling (a theoretician of being as power), culminates in Nietzsche,[12] in agreement with the final pseudo-aphorism of *The Will to Power*:

> And do you know what "the world" is to me? Shall I show it to you in my mirror? This world: a monster of energy, without beginning, without end; a firm, iron magnitude of force that does not grow bigger or smaller, that does not expend itself but only transforms itself [. . .] this, my *Dionysian* world of the eternally self-creating, the eternally self-destroying, this mystery world of the twofold voluptuous delight, my "beyond good and evil," [. . .] do you want a *name* for this world? A *solution* for all its riddles? A *light* for you, too, you best-concealed, strongest, most intrepid, most midnightly men?—*This world is the will to power*—and nothing besides! And you yourselves are also this will to power—and nothing besides![13]

If, then—with a radical postmodernism—we say that the so-called "truth" is a matter of power, we must also add that the true truth, the one without quotation marks, is *not* a matter of power. Otherwise we get into a vicious circle from which it is impossible to escape. In its manifestation *prima facie*, that of the truth as pure power is a very resigned, almost desperate statement: "the reason of the strongest is always the best." And yet we should be more hopeful: reality—for example, the fact that it is true that the wolf is upstream and the lamb is downstream, so it cannot muddy the water—is the very basis for reestablishing justice. For, contrary to what many postmodern thinkers believe, there are reasonable grounds to think, first of all on the basis of the teachings of history, that reality and truth have always constituted the protection of the weak against the oppression of the strong. If, however, a philosopher says that "the so-called 'truth' is a matter of power," then why is he a philosopher rather than a magician?

DIALECTIC

In the fallacy of knowledge-power we are able to measure how influential Nietzsche's philosophy has been; in particular how it managed to ferry elements proper of the romantic reaction to the contemporary world, constituting, as Habermas wrote,[14] a sort of "turning point" that leads from the archaic to the postmodern. Nietzsche's target, from *The Birth of Tragedy* on, was Socrates: the one who, dying, argued that there is an institutive connection between knowledge, virtue, and happiness. And Nietzsche sets against Socrates—a philosopher-scientist, scholar, rationalist, very remote ancestor of the learned positivists of his time—the idea of the tragic philosopher, or of a kind of music-loving Socrates: that is, Wagner. Philosophy must return to the myth, the happiness promised to the scholar must be replaced by tragedy. Here, so to speak, Nietzsche addresses "mother-in-law Socrates" in order to blame "daughter-in-law Enlightenment," because it is precisely Enlightenment that supported the interdependent relationship between knowledge, progress, and happiness. Because the artist-philosopher who loves the veil and the illusion belongs to the same world as Dostoevsky's Grand Inquisitor and shares with him the project of giving humanity what it really needs. And, going back, he also belongs to the world of de Maistre, brilliant slanderer of Enlightenment about what, in his opinion, was most wrong in it, that is, the claim to help people by teaching them to think for themselves, whereas happiness lies in obeying authority and being tied to it with the sweet chains of ignorance and tradition.

With *The Birth of Tragedy*—a really (it must be said) "epoch-making" text, released just over a hundred years before Lyotard's *The Postmodern Condition*—begins the path that leads us to recognize in postmodernism the end of the "great narratives" of Enlightenment, Idealism, and Marxism, which were united by their common acknowledgment of the central role of knowledge in the welfare of humanity. Either because, as in the case of Enlightenment—which remains the paradigmatic element—knowledge leads to emancipation; or because, as in the case of Idealism, knowledge is fully disinterested and disengaged from whatever mundane purpose; or again, as in the case of Marxism, because Enlightenment and Idealism, emancipation and disinterest, are combined in a process of practical transformation of the society. These are the elements questioned by Nietzsche and by the deriving postmodernism. Enlightenment is refuted by the ideal of the tragic philosopher that, as we said, is committed to blowing up every bridge between happiness and knowledge. Idealism is delegitimized by the consideration, fully developed in *On the Genealogy of Morals*, for which knowledge is nothing more than interest, hatred among the learned, and rivalry. The critique of socialism, in Nietzsche, appears as a secondary phenomenon compared to the radical anti-Enlightenment stances, and the argument that "there are no facts, only interpretations" finds its origin exactly in this theoretical horizon: it is important that knowledge is transformed into a series of interpretations that do not match the facts, since one has to follow the model of the artistic thinker, who looks for other masks behind the mask, and not that of the scholar, who seeks the truth behind the veil. The background of the fundamental principle of philosophical postmodernism must therefore be sought in this passage of *The Birth of Tragedy*: "if the artist in every unveiling of truth always cleaves with raptured eyes only to that which still remains veiled after the unveiling, the theoretical man, on the other hand, enjoys and contents himself with the cast-off veil."[15]

It is this passage that echoes in a famous scene in *The Matrix*: "I know this steak doesn't exist. I know that when I put it in my mouth, the Matrix is telling my brain that it is juicy and delicious. After nine years, you know what I realize? Ignorance is bliss." Ignorance is bliss because knowledge and unveiling do not give happiness: it can only come from myth. In Nietzsche echoes the question posed by the Romantics at the beginning of the nineteenth century: how, after two thousand years have passed, have we not even been able to come up with a new God? We have to change everything and give life to a revolution of the heart and of the spirit. As a result (of course, without their direct responsibility), a crowd of charismatic figures came out of it, a new mythology that has long weighed on the last two centuries. Concretely, the colorful, noisy, and especially fake world around us is the heir to the romantic dream of a revival of the myth, to the fact that reason must be replaced by the dream. Rather than rationalistic as it is often depicted, modernity—at least from Romanticism onward—was largely mythological and anti-Enlightenment, and the outcome of post-modernism arises, in full coherence, in this line of development.

It is the theoretical man that must be beaten, but he has to be beaten, mind you (here is the essential dialectic of post-modernism), in the name of truth, which is denied and geared toward myth for the sake of truth itself. Here is the noble origin of the fallacy of knowledge-power. If we look at the philosophical heart of postmodernism, we are faced with an institutive paradox. The basic idea was that of a great emancipatory instance: the request for emancipation, which relies on the forces of reason, knowledge, and truth that are opposed to myth, miracle, and tradition, comes to a point of extreme radicalization and turns against itself.[16] After using the *logos* to criticize myth and knowledge to expose faith, the deconstructive forces of reason turn against the *logos* and knowledge themselves: thus begins the long process of the genealogy of morals, which exposes knowledge as the action of the will to power. The result is exactly the fallacy of knowledge-power: every form of knowledge should be viewed with suspicion, as an expression of some form of power. Hence the impasse: if knowledge is power, then what has to produce emancipation (i.e., knowledge) is at the same time the instance that produces subordination and domination. And that is why, with yet another somersault, the radical emancipation can only be found in nonknowledge, in the return to myth and fables. Thus emancipation went around in circles. For the sake of truth and reality, truth and reality themselves were given up: that is the meaning of the "crisis of the great narratives" of legitimation of knowledge. The problem with this dialectic, however, is simply that it leaves all the initiative to other instances and that emancipation turns into its opposite, as is shown by what happened after.

This dialectic, in fact, has not simply a historical-ideal side, but involves the practical actualizations that we have reviewed in chapter 1. It begins exactly with deconstructive statements, typically with theses that cast doubt on the possibility of an access to the real that is not culturally mediated and that, at the same time, relativize the cognitive value of science, following a thread that leads from Nietzsche and Heidegger to Feyerabend and Foucault. Apart from the case of Heidegger, where the conservative and traditionalist element is widely prevalent, the deconstruction of science and the affirmation of the relativism of conceptual schemes are part of the emancipative baggage that underlies the original postmodern impulse, but their result is diametrically opposed. In particular, as we have seen, the criticism of science as an apparatus of power and as the free play of conceptual schemes generated a conservative postmodernism, one that draws from the dialectic of Enlightenment and from the struggle of truth against itself its argument for the appeal to a higher truth or (and it is the same) to bid truth farewell. This stalemate seems to be a constant outcome of the dialectic of postmodernism:[17] skepticism and deconstruction dismantle philosophical certainties, and the original scene of the Descartes-Kant-Nietzsche arch drawn in chapter 2 is regularly repeated. In this context, it is entirely understandable that there should be a philosophical proposal[18] to offer a way out of the dialectic of postmodernism and the impasse in which finds itself, by acknowledging the positive values of certainty and of a pretheoretical trust that would remedy the syndrome of suspicion, the lacerations of modernism and the nihilism of postmodernism.

CERTAINTY

The prospect of certainty roughly goes like this. We live in a state of uncertainty, which, paradoxically, has been increased, and not diminished, by technical-scientific progress. Modernity, which is the age of the highest knowledge, is also the era of the utmost concern. And this anxiety reached its peak in the second half of the twentieth century, that is, with postmodernism. In order to find security, it is therefore necessary to follow a different path. We should not think that peace will come from objectivity and knowledge (which moreover nail us to our biological dimension and therefore, as the friends of certainty say, to despair). On the contrary, we should focus on certainty and confidence, on relying on others with the trust that a child has toward his mother. It is a discourse that can be lucid, honest, open and deep, but it must be confronted with four perplexities.

Does modernity bring uncertainty? Are we sure? Here is the first question. Think of the lives of our distant ancestors in the savannas: their life lasted roughly twenty years, barely the time to consume their two sets of teeth and then their wisdom teeth as a last resort, and then they faced death from hunger and rheumatism—unless they had been eaten by lions before that. Thus, our ancestors were much more exposed than us, and their life was infinitely shorter and much more cruel, brutal, and senseless than ours. It is in this perspective that faith and knowledge find their very remote origin. In tombs we find technical tools, weapons, and ornaments, as well as religious objects such as statues of gods. These two types of items have evolved in parallel, not to enhance but to decrease uncertainty. However, if we now live in an incomparably safer world and if—trivially but decisively—our lifetime is vastly longer, this does not depend on faith but on knowledge, that therefore, to all purposes, has increased our certainties. And if we are so sensitive to uncertainty it is not due to some failure in modernity, but rather because we have become more civilized and demanding, in a process similar to that for which today we would not bear the surgeries undergone by our ancestors without anesthesia.

Emotional security or objective certainty? The second question is: are we sure that (as the friends of certainty claim) the first certainty we have is not objectivity but the fact of our dependence on our mother for affection? Some people have never met their mother, while objects are known by all, and the relationship of trust between the child and the mother is itself primarily established as an objectual relationship. That said, it is true that certainty is something that—like courage according to Don Abbondio—one does not give oneself but that is received. But, again, we continuously receive it from the world, which is stable and reliable in front of us. The observation that we are the more certain the less we have set reasoning in motion is sacrosanct.[19] But such a remark is intimately connected with objective experience, because otherwise we would be expressing the *credo quia absurdum*, or even a blind submission to authority.

Certainty or hope? The third question is: are we certain that certainty is the highest good? In the final analysis, depression is the closest human experience to eternal peace and absolute certainty. This is what makes even the representation of eternal life unsatisfactory and unexplainable, when we try to fixate it in a more definite way. Something much stronger and much more decisive than certainty is hope (which always has an internal element of uncertainty), as is intuitively clear if we compare the different severity of their opposites, that is, uncertainty and despair. There is no reason to believe that a human being, if she renounces a transcendent order, must necessarily surrender to despair. In fact, hope precedes every religious revelation and may evolve to become a rational hope valid for all people, that is, a hope that does not contradict what we know of our natural being, unlike what happens for the hope, valid only for believers, of resurrection.[20]

Certainty or truth? And here we come to a crucial fourth uncertainty. Are we certain that we can be certain of certainty?

Should we trust it? There are bad mothers, both in the literal sense and figuratively; there are deceivers and manipulators, both in the name of reason and in the name of faith. Moreover, certainty (and sensible experience itself proves it) can be deceitful. So, I can have hallucinations, or my mother might not be my mother, or even—as happened to the boys of the Hitlerjugend—my certainty and my fundamental reliance could be named Adolf Hitler. So, certainty alone is not enough: it needs truth, that is, knowledge. Here, rather than with the experience of the reliance on the mother, we are confronted with a different movement, namely, with man's emergence from childhood and with the "dare to know" brought forward by Enlightenment. In fact, no one denies that in the light of reliance, certainty, and dependence, one can live and die—maybe even very well. And of course Oedipus would have lived better had he not found out the truth. Yet, these practical or rather "eudemonistic" motives (to use an old-fashioned expression) do not exempt us from a consideration: living in certainty, for what we have said so far, is not living in truth. And we should note that it is in the name of truth that the promise of certainty—maybe the "worship, rejoice, be silent" with which a great philosopher, Antonio Rosmini, ended his earthly life—gives peace. But it is also true that peace, as Kafka said, "would be of a kind desirable only for one's ashes."[21]

ENLIGHTENMENT

So let us come to the alternative to Enlightenment. We have seen a possible outcome of the dialectic of postmodernism—the one leading to the fallacy of knowledge-power and hence to antifoundationalism and then again to a non-theoretical neofoundationalism—in order to circumvent the objection of knowledge-power. But there is one aspect of the recent history of postmodernism on which I would like to bring attention: in the early eighties—and in front of the turn postmodernism was taking—three philosophers who were systematically associated with postmodernism (namely, Foucault, Derrida, and Lyotard) expressed the need for a return to Enlightenment. It is typically the case of Lyotard, who in 1983, with an open disassociation from the path taken by postmodernism, proposed a return to Kant:[22] this was the main theme of his last works, in which, for example, he focused on the sublime as opposed to the cultural industry.[23] The same passage may be noted in Derrida, who (in 1980, at the conference in Cerisy-la-Salle in his honor) entitled his speech, where he targeted the signs of the "end of an era" that accompanied the debate on postmodernism, *Of an Apocalyptic Tone Recently Adopted in Philosophy*.[24] Over the years he would increase his interventions in favor of an "Enlightenment to come" and the "Enlightenment of the XXI century."[25] "The currents that call themselves 'postmodern'"—wrote Derrida—"do so as if they had passed the age of Enlightenment, and I do not think it is so. It is a matter of reviving the idea of Enlightenment, not as it manifested itself in the eighteenth century in Europe, but by making it contemporary, situating it in the *progress of reason*."[26]

But in this respect, the most emblematic case is that of Foucault, who from February 1 to March 28, 1984 held his last course at the Collège de France, *The Courage of the Truth*,[27] and then entered the terminal stage of AIDS that would take him away on June 25. Foucault was tired; the course began with weeks of delay because of a strong flu due to his immunodeficiency, but he wanted to complete the task that was assigned to him the year before: to carry out a history of parrhesia, that is, telling the truth at the cost of one's life, from its birth in Greece to its developments in the Middle Ages (the sermon and the university) up to modern times, where the parrhesiast seems to turn into the figure of the revolutionary. For the philosopher who had linked his name to the doctrine of knowledge-power, that is, to the idea that one has to look at knowledge with suspicion because it is a vehicle for power, this project—just like the rehabilitation of asceticism and self-care in *The History of Sexuality* that is Foucault's great unfinished work—is the sign of a profound change of direction. From the very first lesson Foucault states that interpreting his research "as an attempt to reduce knowledge (savoir) to power [. . .] is purely and simply a caricature."[28] Yet, the dramatic interplay between power and knowledge was the first motive of Foucault's thought, as is once again restated in "The Order of Discourse,"[29] the lecture with which, in 1970, he inaugurated his teaching at the Collège de France. And it is still so in the synthesis of the "Microphysics of Power": "the exercise of power perpetually creates knowledge and, conversely, knowledge constantly induces effects of power."[30]

As we have seen, the theory of knowledge-power harbored a reincarnation of *On the Genealogy of Morals* and established a paradox that lies at the heart of Foucault's thought as well as Nietzsche's: truth is criticized not for the sake of mystification but for the opposite reason, namely, for a love for truth that wants to unmask everything, including truth itself, thus restoring myth. A dangerous game, because seeing truth as an effect of power means delegitimizing the tradition culminating in Enlightenment, for which knowledge and truth are vehicles of emancipation, tools of counterpower and virtue. And an unpredictable game, too, like Russian roulette, because one cannot know when it ends. For Nietzsche, the outcome is the myth, the idea that truth must give way to illusion and the unfolding of power. For Foucault, the outcome is antithetical. In fact, it is no coincidence that, along with this apology of truth as a critique of, and an opposition to, power, a truth that costs one's life or that is embodied by cynics as opponents of power, Foucault engages in an apology of Enlightenment, as happens in a lecture at the Collège de France in 1983, "What Is Enlightenment?"[31]

This is the path that was completed in the lectures of the last winter of Foucault's life, where the terminal hero is the dying Socrates, that is, the antihero in Nietzsche, who regarded him as the man who, dying, had imposed the false equation between knowledge, virtue, and happiness. For Foucault, instead, Socrates is the parrhesiast *par excellence*, unlike the scientist who does not speak in the first person, unlike the sophist who wants to win the argument and convince, unlike the prophet who speaks in the name of God, and unlike the wise man who says the truth in secluded places. Socrates wants to tell the truth, as a personal testimony, in public and at the cost of his own life.

The climax of the course is the lecture of February 22, dedicated to the death of Socrates, which ends with these words: "As a philosophy professor one really must have lectured on Socrates and the death of Socrates at least once in one's life. It's done. *Salvate animam meam.*"[32] Save my soul. The invocation is ironic, as always in Foucault, who even in these lectures could make jokes leaving us a glimpse of his dazed laughter, but the theme is not at all ironic. Because Socrates, for Foucault, is the one for whom the unexamined life is worthless,[33] and who now represents the quintessence of the risk of a truth that makes us free and not slaves.

I believe that at least one lesson can be drawn from this intellectual story. As dissimilar from one another as they are, thinkers such as Lyotard, Derrida, and Foucault—precisely those that come to mind when one thinks of the philosophical fathers of postmodernism (although the first one was more like its Baptist in philosophy, and the other two never declared themselves postmodernists)—are the expression of a radical Enlightenment or, if you wish, of a dialectic of Enlightenment, namely, of the paradox that I set out earlier in this chapter.

This is why, without contradictions, they could be the inspiration for a movement that has evolved in conservative and anti-Enlightenment terms while, at the same time, ending up legitimately defending the Enlightenment emancipative instance. It is obvious that one can continue, if one wishes, to repeat even today the watchwords of the hyper-deconstructionist Derrida who in the seventies claimed that nothing exists outside the text; or that one can insist, this time with the Foucault anterior to the rethinking of *The Will to Knowledge*, that the world is merely the outcome of our conceptual schemes. But perhaps, at least if we keep the emancipative spirit that animated the work of these authors, it is better to try not to close our eyes to the regressive outcome of the dialectic of postmodernism and renew its teaching in the sense of a new Enlightenment rather than that of an old obscurantism.

Liberation

So we return to where we started, to *The Postmodern Condition*. Lyotard's analysis, which was not at all a defense of the postmodern Brave New World, had the merit of identifying the risks of this ideological collapse loaded with practical consequences, from the severe cuts to university funding wanted by Margaret Thatcher in England to the globalization of the free market, which became truly global after 1989. The result, in the nineties, was that the "IE" of Idealism and Enlightenment was transformed into the "IEB" of Internet, English, and Business, with an attitude that was shared not only by center-right governments that wanted cuts to culture and basic research but also by many intellectuals, who became skeptics of their own mission and were probably influenced (or, rather, justified) by the fallacy of knowledge-power. We also examined the two possible reactions to the fallacy: the one that relies on certainty and the one that focuses on emancipation. I think it is best to live up to what was important and alive in postmodernism, that is, the demand for emancipation, which starts from Socrates's ideal of the moral value of knowledge and is stated more precisely in Kant's discourse on Enlightenment—perhaps the most maligned among the categories of thought,[34] deserving a new voice in the contemporary intellectual scene in front of the consequences of the fallacy of knowledge-power.

We learn from our mistakes, or at least others learn. Bidding truth farewell is not only a gift we give to "Power" without a countergift but mostly the withdrawal of the only chance of emancipation that is given to humankind, that is, realism, against illusion and sorcery. Here is the importance of knowledge: here lies the correction—always possible and therefore dutiful—of the "crooked timber of humanity" and the choice not to resign to be minors (regardless of our chronological age); even though, as Kant wrote, it is so comfortable to be minors. Rejecting man's emergence from childhood, perhaps under the pretense of revealing the collusion between knowledge and power, is certainly possible, but it means choosing the always open alternative proposed by the Grand Inquisitor: that of taking the path of miracles, mystery, and authority.

NOTES

PROLOGUE

1. Unlike, for instance, an earlier "new realism" that was a post-idealist current at the start of the twentieth century (see Edwin B. Holt, Walter T. Marvin, William Pepperrell Montague, Ralph Barton Perry, and Edward Gleason Spaulding, *The New Realism: Cooperative Studies in Philosophy* [New York: Macmillan, 1912]). For a programmatic presentation, see "The Program and First Platform of Six Realists," in *The Journal of Philosophy, Psychology and Scientific Methods* 7, 18 (1910): 393–401. For the contemporary uses of the term "realism," see "Realism" in *Stanford Encyclopedia of Philosophy*, http://plato.stanford.edu/entries/realism/.
2. For a comment on this I refer the reader back to my article "Nuovo realismo FAQ," in *Noema: Rivista online di filosofia*, http://riviste.unimi.it/index.php/noema/article/view/1403. The full press review on new realism can be found on http://nuovorealismo.wordpress.com/.

3. *La Repubblica*, 8 August 2011.
4. For a general overview, see my "Autopresentazione," in Dario Antiseri and Silvano Tagliagambe, eds., *Filosofi italiani contemporanei* (Milan: Bompiani, 2009), 226–235.
5. Hilary Putnam, *Renewing Philosophy* (Cambridge, MA: Harvard University Press, 1992), 133.

CHAPTER 1. REALITISM

1. Jean-François Lyotard, *The Postmodern Condition: A Report on Knowledge* (Minneapolis: University of Minnesota Press, 1984 [1979]).
2. For the origins and the development of postmodernism I refer the reader back to the analyses I proposed in *Tracce: Nichilismo moderno postmoderno* (Milan: Mimesis, 2006 [1983]), with a new afterword, "Postmoderno vent'anni dopo," 165–171.
3. "Against positivism, which halts at phenomena—'There are only *facts*'—I would say: No, facts are precisely what there is not, only interpretations. We cannot establish any fact 'in itself': perhaps it is folly to want to do such a thing. 'Everything is subjective,' you say; but even this is interpretation. The 'subject' is not something given, it is something added and invented and projected behind what there is.—Finally, is it necessary to posit an interpreter behind the interpretation? Even this is invention, hypothesis. Insofar as the word 'knowledge' has any meaning, the world is knowable; but it is *interpretable* otherwise, it has no meaning behind it, but countless meanings.—'Perspectivism.' It is our needs that interpret the world; our drives and their For and Against. Every drive is a kind of lust to rule; each one has its perspective that it would like to compel all the

other drives to accept as a norm." Friedrich Nietzsche, *The Will to Power* (New York: Vintage Books, 1967), §481.

4. Richard Rorty, *Contingency, Irony, and Solidarity* (Cambridge, UK: Cambridge University Press, 1989).
5. Gilles Deleuze and Félix Guattari, *Anti-Oedipus: Capitalism and Schizophrenia* (Minneapolis: University of Minnesota Press, 1983 [1972]).
6. Richard Rorty, *Solidarity or Objectivity?* (1984), in Michael Krausz, ed., *Relativism: Interpretation and Confrontation* (Notre Dame: University of Notre Dame Press, 1989).
7. These are the two common assumptions of the two founding texts of philosophical postmodernism, namely, the already mentioned *Postmodern Condition* by Lyotard and Richard Rorty, *Philosophy and the Mirror of Nature* (Princeton: Princeton University Press, 1979).
8. Roland Barthes, *Leçon* (Paris: Éditions du Seuil, 1978).
9. Richard Rorty, "Philosophy as a Kind of Writing" (1978), in Richard Rorty, *The Consequences of Pragmatism* (Minneapolis: University of Minnesota Press, 1982), 90–109.
10. After all, irony, in rhetoric, is an allusive proceeding for reducing to mockery real data, by mystifying them: in fact, both in ancient Greek (*eironéia*) and in Latin (*simulatio*), the terms designating the trope mean "fiction," "deceit."
11. Gilles Deleuze, *Difference and Repetition* (New York: Columbia University Press, 1995 [1968]).
12. In *Theatrum Philosophicum*, the review of *Difference and Repetition* originally appeared in "Critique" and was later published as a foreword to the Italian edition.
13. I have analyzed this aspect in *Goodbye Kant! What Still Stands of the "Critique of Pure Reason,"* translated by Richard Davies (Albany: State University of New York Press, 2013).
14. Gianni Vattimo and Pier Aldo Rovatti, eds., *Il pensiero*

debole (Milan: Feltrinelli, 1983); English translation: *Weak Thought*, trans. and with an introduction by Peter Carravetta (Albany: State University of New York Press, 2012).

15. Carlo Augusto Viano, *Va' pensiero: Il carattere della filosofia italiana contemporanea* (Turin: Einaudi, 1985).
16. Joseph Marie comte de Maistre, *The Pope: Considered in His Relations with the Church, Temporal Sovereignties, Separated Churches, and the Cause of Civilization* (London: C. Dolman, 1850), 79.
17. Immanuel Kant, *An Answer to the Question: "What Is Enlightenment?"* (London: Penguin, 2010).
18. Dario Antiseri and Gianni Vattimo, *Ragione filosofica e fede religiosa nell'era postmoderna* (Soveria Mannelli: Rubbettino, 2008).
19. Martin Heidegger, "Nur noch ein Gott kann uns retten," *Spiegel* 30 (May 1976): 193–219, trans. William Richardson as "Only a God Can Save Us," in Thomas Sheehan, ed., *Heidegger: The Man and the Thinker* (Chicago: Precedent, 1981), 45–67.
20. In this prevailing version, the adhesion to Nazism was presented as "one of those things," which was already over by 1934 (precisely in accordance with Heidegger's self-defense), and the Heideggerian texts circulating among left-wingers were certainly not the Rectorial Address but seemingly more innocuous texts in which he stated that language is the home of being and that poetically man dwells. Of course, there too were some disquieting bits, for instance, in a 1940 course on Nietzsche, there is praise of the ongoing *Blitzkrieg* or, again in the *Spiegel* interview, the thesis according to which the Shoah had to be placed on the same level as the mechanization of agriculture.
21. Martin Heidegger, *Scritti politici* (1933–1936) (Casale Monferrato: Piemme, 1998), 329.
22. "Yes, my friends, believe with me in Dionysian life and

in the re-birth of tragedy. The time of the Socratic man is past: crown yourselves with ivy, take in your hands the thyrsus, and do not marvel if tigers and panthers lie down fawning at your feet. Dare now to be tragic men, for ye are to be redeemed! Ye are to accompany the Dionysian festive procession from India to Greece! Equip yourselves for severe conflict, but believe in the wonders of your god!" Friedrich Nietzsche, "The Birth of Tragedy," in *The Complete Works of Friedrich Nietzsche*, ed. Oscar Levy (London: George Allen & Unwin, 1923), 157.

23. Marco Belpoliti, *Il corpo del capo* (Parma: Guanda, 2009).
24. Richard Wagner, *Art and Revolution* (Whitefish, MO: Kessinger, 2010 [1849]).
25. Max Horkheimer and Theodor W. Adorno, *Dialectic of Enlightenment: Philosophical Fragments* (Stanford: Stanford University Press, 2002 [1947]).
26. Michel Foucault, *The Will to Knowledge* (London: Penguin, 1991 [1976]).
27. Jürgen Habermas, *The Structural Transformation of the Public Sphere: An Inquiry into a Category of Bourgeois Society* (Cambridge: MIT Press, 1991 [1962]).
28. Michel Foucault, "Nietzsche, Genealogy, History," in *The Foucault Reader*, ed. Paul Rabinow (Harmondsworth: Penguin, 1984), 87–90.
29. Manfred Frank, *Der kommende Gott: Vorlesungen über die Neue Mythologie* (Frankfurt am Main: Suhrkamp, 1982).
30. Paul K. Feyerabend, *Wider den Methodenzwang* (Frankfurt am Main: Suhrkamp, 1975), 206: "The church at the time of Galileo was much more faithful to reason than Galileo himself, and also took into consideration the ethical and social consequences of Galileo's doctrine. Its verdict against Galileo was rational and just, and revisionism can be legitimized solely for motives of political opportunism."

31. Joseph Ratzinger, *A Turning Point for Europe?* (San Francisco: Ignatius Press, 2010), 101–105.
32. This thesis, which I presented in "Dal postmoderno al populismo," in *Alfabeta2* 2 (September 2010) and in *Ricostruire la decostruzione: Cinque saggi a partire da Jacques Derrida* (Milan: Bompiani, 2010), can also be found in Valerio Magrelli, *Il Sessantotto realizzato da Mediaset* (Turin: Einaudi, 2011) and in Mario Perniola, *Berlusconi o il '68 realizzato* (Milan: Mimesis, 2011).
33. Ron Suskind, "Faith, Certainty and the Presidency of George W. Bush," *New York Times Magazine* (17 October 2004).
34. Jean Baudrillard, *Art and Artefact* (London: Sage, 1997).
35. Maurizio Ferraris, "Benvenuti nel realitysmo," *La Repubblica* (29 January 2011), to which I here partly refer.
36. Richard Rorty, "The World Well Lost," *Journal of Philosophy* 69, 19 (1972): 649–665. Moreover, the title of Rorty's article was taken from a sci-fi short story by Theodore Sturgeon.
37. Thomas Reid, *The Works of Thomas Reid*, vol.1 (Charlestown: Samuel Etheridge, 1813), 169.
38. Which Žižek repeats twice in *Living in the End Times* (London: Verso, 2010). See my discussion "Il segno di Žižek," *Alfalibri*, supplement of *Alfabeta2* 12 (September 2011): 2–3.
39. The turn from metaphysical realism to internal realism (which is much more open to relativism) happened in Putnam precisely in the years of postmodernism, that is, between *Meaning and the Moral Sciences* (London: Routledge and Kegan Paul, 1978) and *Reason, Truth, and History* (Cambridge: Cambridge University Press, 1981); the new realistic perspectives can be seen in *Renewing Philosophy* (Cambridge, MA: Harvard University Press, 1992).

For an excellent presentation of Putnam's path through realism, see Mario De Caro, "Il lungo viaggio di Hilary Putnam: Realismo metafisico, antirealismo e realismo naturale," *Lingua e stile* 4 (1996): 527–545.

40. Umberto Eco, *Kant e l'ornitorinco* (Milan: Bompiani, 1997), but already Umberto Eco, *I limiti dell'interpretazione* (Milan: Bompiani, 1990).
41. See Quentin Meillassoux, *Après la finitude: Essai sur la nécessité de la contingence* (Paris: Seuil, 2006); Ray Brassier, *Nihil Unbound: Enlightenment and Extinction* (London: Palgrave Macmillan, 2007); Markus Gabriel, *Transcendental Ontology: Essays in German Idealism* (New York, London: Continuum, 2011), Markus Gabriel, *Il senso dell'esistenza: Disegno di un'ontologia iperrealista* (Rome: Carrocci, 2012). See also Levi Bryant, Nick Srnicek, and Graham Harman, eds., *The Speculative Turn: Continental Materialism and Realism* (Melbourne: re.press, 2011).
42. I refer the reader to my *Estetica razionale* (Milan: Raffaello Cortina, 2011 [1997]); but for an overall analysis, see Paolo D'Angelo, *Estetica* (Rome and Bari: Laterza, 2011).
43. A vast treatise on this turn can be found in my edited collection *Storia dell'ontologia* (Milan: Bompiani, 2008).
44. Immanuel Kant, *Critique of Pure Reason* (1781–1787) (Edinburgh: Henry G. Bohn, 1855), A 247/B 303.
45. Charles Baudelaire, *Mon coeur mis à nu*, XIII: "Vous figurez-vous un Dandy parlant au peuple, excepté pour le bafouer?"
46. Jürgen Habermas, "Die Moderne / ein unvollendetes Projekt," in *KleinePolitische Schriften* (Frankfurt am Main: Suhrkamp, 1981), 444–464.
47. Charles Baudelaire, *Fusées*, II.
48. Kant, *An Answer to the Question: "What Is Enlightenment?"* §1.

CHAPTER 2. REALISM

1. Diego Marconi, "Il postmoderno ucciso dalle sue caricature," *La Repubblica* (3 December 2011). On the subject of realism and antirealism, see also his *Per la verità: Relativismo e filosofia* (Turin: Einaudi, 2007).
2. Immanuel Kant, *Critique of Pure Reason* (1781–1787) (Edinburgh: Henry G. Bohn, 1855), A 51/B 75: "Thoughts without content are empty, intuitions without concepts are blind."
3. For a deeper analysis, I refer the reader to my *Goodbye Kant! What Still Stands of the "Critique of Pure Reason,"* translated by Richard Davies (Albany: State University of New York Press, 2013).
4. See ibid., 43–48.
5. René Descartes, *Discourse on Method and Metaphysical Meditations*, trans. G. B. Rawlings (London and Felling-On-Tyne: The Walter Scott Publishing Co.,1901 [1641]), First meditation, §§3–4.
6. Alfredo Ferrarin, "Construction and Mathematical Schematism: Kant on the Exhibition of a Concept in Intuition," *Kant-Studien* 86 (1995): 131–174.
7. The meaning of this nonconceptual "encounter" is clarified in the section "Amendable and Unamendable" of this chapter.
8. "As the archaeology of our thought easily shows, man is an invention of recent date. And one perhaps nearing its end. If those arrangements were to disappear as they appeared, if some event of which we can at the moment do no more than sense the possibility—without knowing either what its form will be or what it promises—were to cause them to crumble, as the ground of Classical thought did, at the end of the eighteenth century, then one can certainly wager that man would be erased, like a face drawn in sand at the

edge of the sea." Michel Foucault, *The Order of Things* (London and New York: Routledge Classics, 2005), 422.

9. See Alan Sokal and Jean Bricmont, *Intellectual Impostures* (London: Profile Books, 2003 [1997]). More on sophisticated *fashionable nonsense* can be found in Paul Boghossian, *Fear of Knowledge: Against Relativism and Constructivism* (New York: Oxford University Press, 2006).
10. I describe this academic skepticism in *Una Ikea di università* (Milan: Raffaello Cortina, 2009 [2001]).
11. Bruno Latour, "Ramses II est-il mort de la tuberculose?" *Recherche* 307 (March 1998): 84–85. Latour has also had the merit of thoroughly revising his positions, as well as hyper-constructionist positions in general, in an admirable article: "Why Has Critique Run Out of Steam? From Matters of Fact to Matters of Concern," *Critical Inquiry* 30 (Autumn 2004): 225–248.
12. I have articulated the distinction between ontology and epistemology in *Il mondo esterno* (Milan: Bompiani, 2001) and in *Documentality: Why It Is Necessary to Leave Traces* (New York: Fordham University Press, 2012), to which I refer the reader.
13. See typically John McDowell, *Mind and World* (Cambridge, MA: Harvard University Press, 1994). For a critique, I refer the reader to my "Mente e mondo o scienza ed esperienza?" *Rivista di estetica* n.s., 12 (2000): 3–77.
14. For instance John Searle, *The Construction of Social Reality* (New York: Free Press, 1995), especially 127ff.
15. Robert Nozick, *Invariances: The Structure of the Objective World* (Cambridge, MA: Harvard University Press, 2001).
16. Ludwig Wittgenstein, *Philosophical Investigations* (Oxford: Blackwell, 2010), §217.
17. John Locke, *An Essay Concerning Human Understanding* (London: Buffet, 1689), IV.2.14.

18. From this point of view, as for my research, the text to start from is *Analogon rationis* (Milan: Pratica filosofica, 1994). For a comprehensive presentation of the role of perception in my perspective, I refer the reader to the afterword of the new edition of my *Estetica razionale* (Milan: Raffaello Cortina, 2011 [1997]), 573–586.
19. Maurizio Ferraris, "Metzger, Kant, and the Perception of Causality," in Johan C. Marek and Maria E. Reicher, eds., *Erfahrung und Analyse* (Wien: ÖBV & HPT, 2005), 297–309. The closeness of Metzger's concept of "encountered" and my concept of "unamendable" has been underlined by Giovanni Bruno Vicario, *Psicologia generale: I fondamenti* (Rome and Bari: Laterza, 2001), 101. I also refer the reader to Vicario's analyses for a presentation of the concept of "reality" in psychology.
20. See Paolo Bozzi, *Fisica ingenua* (Milan: Garzanti, 1990); Paolo Bozzi, *Scritti sul realismo* (Milan: Mimesis, 2007) (I argue more extensively what I am saying here in the introduction to that volume, 11–20; for the ontological implications, I refer the reader to my "Ontologia come Fisica ingenua," *Rivista di estetica* n.s., 6 [1998]: 133–143).
21. And as I articulated in *Il mondo esterno*, 198–201.
22. See ibid., 89 ff., to which I refer the reader for a complete phenomenology.
23. For a more detailed analysis, see ibid., 193–201.

Chapter 3. Reconstruction

1. TN: Typical Italian expression, which some say dates back to Roman times, that is paradigmatic of the attitude that blames the government for everything, even natural events.
2. Jacques Derrida, *Force de loi* (Paris: Galilée, 1994), 35 ff.
3. It was proposed and developed in *Ricostruire la*

decostruzione; the model of the experiment is, obviously, Hilary Putnam, "Brains in a Vat," in *Reason, Truth, and History* (Cambridge, UK: Cambridge University Press, 1981), 1– 22.

4. This is the difference between my perspective and the approach of Bozzi, Moore, and all naïve realists. Of "moderate realism" spoke Philip Kitcher, *Science, Truth, and Democracy* (Oxford: Oxford University Press, 2001).
5. See Aldo Giorgio Gargani, "L'attrito del pensiero," in Gianni Vattimo, ed., *Filosofia '86* (Rome and Bari: Laterza, 1987), 5–22. The metaphor comes from Wittgenstein: "We have got on to slippery ice where there is no friction and so in a certain sense the conditions are ideal, but also, just because of that, we are unable to walk. We want to walk: so we need *friction*. Back to the rough ground!" Wittgenstein, *Philosophical Investigations* (Oxford: Blackwell, 2010), §107.
6. Primo Levi, *"If This Is a Man" and "The Truce"* (London: Penguin, 1979), 188.
7. Quentin Meillassoux, *Après la finitude: Essai sur la nécessité de la contingence* (Paris: Seuil, 2006).
8. On this topic I refer the reader to my "Necessità materiale," in *Le parole dell'Essere* (Milan: Bruno Mondadori, 2005), 231–257.
9. In accordance with the so-called Tarskian biconditional: "'The snow is white' is true if and only if snow is white."
10. Ian Hacking, *The Social Construction of What?* (Cambridge, MA: Harvard University Press, Cambridge, 1999), 1.
11. Edward Said, *Orientalism* (London: Penguin, 1977).
12. On the need to discuss this case-by-case (which is precisely the opposite of a maximalist solution like "everything is socially constructed"), I refer the reader to my dialogue with Achille C. Varzi, "Che cosa c'è e che cos'è," *Nous*

(2004): 81–101, later reelaborated in Achille C. Varzi, *Il mondo messo a fuoco: Storie di allucinazioni e miopie filosofiche* (Rome and Bari: Laterza, 2010).

13. On the thematization of social objects and social ontology as a whole, I refer the reader to my *Where Are You? An Ontology of the Cell Phone* (New York: Fordham University Press, 2014), *Documentality: Why It Is Necessary to Leave Traces* (New York: Fordham University Press, 2012), and *Anima e iPad* (Parma: Guanda, 2011).
14. "Il n'y a pas de hors-texte," literally (and asemantically), "there is no outside-text," see Jacques Derrida, *Of Grammatology* (Baltimore: Johns Hopkins University Press, 1998), 58.
15. Ernst Jünger, "Total Mobilization," in Richard Wolin, ed., *The Heidegger Controversy: A Critical Reader* (Cambridge: MIT Press, 1993), 119–129.
16. Once again, I refer the reader to *Anima e iPad*, 59–84.
17. Explained in Maurizio Ferraris, *Ricostruire la decostruzione: Cinque saggi a partire da Jacques Derrida* (Milan: Bompiani, 2010), 79–97.
18. The role of collective intentionality in Searle's social ontology has grown over the years. I have discussed this problematic evolution in *Anima e iPad*, 96–101.
19. "It is, for example, a mistake to treat money and other such instruments as if they were natural phenomena like the phenomena studied in physics, chemistry, and biology. The recent economic crisis makes it clear that they are products of massive fantasy." John Searle, *Making the Social World: The Structure of Human Civilization* (Oxford: Oxford University Press, 2010), 201.
20. For an elaboration, see *Documentality*, parts 4 and 5.
21. "The breeding of an animal that *can promise*—is not this just the very paradox of a task which nature has set itself

in regard to man?" Friedrich Nietzsche, *The Genealogy of Morals* (Minneola: Courier Dover Publications, 2003), 34.

22. I developed this aspect in *Anima e iPad*, 144ff.; see also Giuliano Torrengo, "Documenti e intenzioni: La documentalità nel dibattito contemporaneo sull'ontologia sociale," *Rivista di estetica* n.s., 42 (2009): 157–188.
23. Daniel Dennett, *Consciousness Explained* (London: Penguin, 1991). Similar insights can be found in the notion of "superorganism" (for example, a family of termites, which exhibits a rational behavior even if none of its components is able to think), see Bert Hölldobler and Edward O. Wilson, *The Superorganism: The Beauty, Elegance, and Strangeness of Insect Societies* (New York: W. W. Norton, 2009).

Chapter 4. Emancipation

1. Jean-Jacques Rousseau, *Discours (. . .) Si le rétablissement des Sciences et desArts a contribué à épurer les moeurs* (1750), in *Oeuvres Complètes* (Paris: Gallimard, 1959–1995), III: 19.
2. On this, see Jürgen Habermas, *Knowledge and Human Interests* (Boston: Beacon Press, 1971 [1968]).
3. For a presentation of this aspect, I refer the reader to the analysis proposed in my *Storia dell'ermeneutica* (Milan: Bompiani, 2008 [1988]), 185–203.
4. Michel Foucault, *History of Madness* (London and New York: Routledge, 2006 [1961]).
5. Michel Foucault, *The Order of Things: An Archaeology of the Human Sciences* (London and New York, Routledge, 2002).
6. Michel Foucault, *Discipline and Punish: The Birth of the Prison* (London and New York: Vintage, 1977).

7. Widely and usefully illustrated by Paolo Rossi, *Paragone degli ingegni moderni e postmoderni* (Bologna: il Mulino, 1989) (new expanded edition, with other examples of this mechanical application of knowledge-power, Bologna: il Mulino, 2009). In fact, even just by observing the university departments in which the theorists of knowledge-power worked (no need to look for exotic worlds), it should be noted there are frequent cases of wise and completely powerless people, as well as powerful people that are far from omniscient.
8. Gianni Vattimo, *A Farewell to Truth* (New York: Columbia University Press, 2011).
9. Pascal Engel and Richard Rorty, *What's the Use of Truth?* (New York: Columbia University Press, 2007).
10. I owe this observation to my friend Enrico Terrone.
11. Georg Lukács, *The Destruction of Reason* (London: Merlin Press, 1980 [1954]).
12. I analyzed Nietzsche's ontology in *Guida a Nietzsche: Etica, politica, filologia, musica, teoria dell'interpretazione, ontologia* (Rome and Bari: Laterza, 2004 [1999]), 199–275.
13. Friedrich Nietzsche, *The Will to Power* (New York: Random House, 2011 [1906]), 550.
14. Jürgen *Habermas*, "The Entry into Postmodernity: Nietzsche as a Turning Point," in *The Philosophical Discourse of Modernity* (Cambridge: MIT Press, 1991 [1985]).
15. Friedrich Nietzsche, *Birth of Tragedy, or Hellenism and Pessimism* (London: George Allen & Unwin, 1909), 115.
16. Max Horkheimer and Theodor W. Adorno, *Dialectic of Enlightenment: Philosophical Fragments* (Stanford: Stanford University Press, 2002 [1947]), 11: "Enlightenment, understood in the widest sense as the advance of thought, has always aimed at liberating human beings from fear and installing them as masters. Yet the wholly enlightened earth is radiant with triumphant calamity."

17. I analyzed these dynamics in more detail in "Il pensiero debole e i suoi rischi," in Elisabetta Ambrosi, ed., *Il bello del relativismo: Quel che resta della filosofia nel XXI secolo* (Venice: Marsilio, 2005), 49–57.
18. Costantino Esposito, "E l'esistenza diventa una immensa certezza," in Emanuela Belloni and Alberto Savorana, eds., *Una certezza per l'esistenza* (Milan: Rizzoli, 2011), 42–66.
19. John Henry Newman, *An Essay in Aid of a Grammar of Assent* (London: Forgotten Books, 2010 [1870]).
20. I extensively discuss this topic in *Babbo Natale, Gesù adulto: In cosa crede chi crede?* (Milan: Bompiani, 2006).
21. Franz Kafka, "16 October 1917," in *Letters to Felice* (London: Secker & Warburg, 1967), 547.
22. Jean-François Lyotard, *The Differend* (Minneapolis: University of Minnesota Press, 1988 [1983]).
23. As in Jean-François Lyotard, "Intervento italiano," *Alfabeta* 32 (January 1982), republished in *Alfabeta2* 14 (November 2011): 9–11.
24. Jacques Derrida, "Of an Apocalyptic Tone Recently Adopted in Philosophy," in Peter Fenves, ed., *Raising the Tone of Philosophy: Late Essays by Immanuel Kant, Transformative Critique by Jacques Derrida* (Baltimore: Johns Hopkins University Press, 1993), 117–171.
25. On Enlightenment in Derrida, I refer the reader to my *Introduzione a Derrida* (Rome and Bari: Laterza, 2003), in particular 95 ff., and *Jackie Derrida, Ritratto a memoria* (Turin: Bollati Boringhieri, 2006), 71 ff..
26. "La Jornada," Mexico City, May 3, 2002, my emphasis.
27. Michel Foucault, *The Courage of the Truth: Lectures at the Collège de France, 1982– 1983* (London: Palgrave Macmillan, 2011).
28. Ibid., 8–9.
29. Foucault, *The Order of Things.*
30. Michel Foucault, *Power/Knowledge: Selected Interviews*

and Other Writings by Michel Foucault, 1972–1977 (New York: Pantheon Books), 52.

31. Michel Foucault, "What Is Enlightenment?" trans. Catherine Porter, in Paul Rabinow, ed., *The Foucault Reader* (New York: Pantheon Books, 1984), 32–50.
32. Foucault, *The Courage of the Truth*, 153.
33. "And if I say again that the greatest good of man is daily to converse about virtue, and all that concerning which you hear me examining myself and others, and that the life which is unexamined is not worth living—that you are still less likely to believe. And yet what I say is true, although a thing of which it is hard for me to persuade you." Plato, *Apology of Socrates*, 38a. It is this passage that echoes in Robert Nozick, *The Examined Life* (New York: Simon & Schuster, 1989).
34. Vincenzo Ferrone, *Lezioni illuministiche* (Rome and Bari: Laterza, 2010). On the rebirth, also theoretical, of Enlightenment, see Jonathan Israel, *A Revolution of the Mind: Radical Enlightenment and the Intellectual Origins of Modern Democracy* (Princeton: Princeton University Press, 2009).

INDEX